Controversies
in Macroeconomics

Controversies in Macroeconomics

K A Chrystal
University of Essex

Second edition

Philip Allan

First published 1979 by

PHILIP ALLAN PUBLISHERS LIMITED
MARKET PLACE
DEDDINGTON
OXFORD OX5 4SE

© K A Chrystal 1979, 1983
All rights reserved

Reprinted 1980, 1982
Second edition 1983

British Library Cataloguing in Publication Data

Chrystal, K. A.
 Controversies in macroeconomics. — 2nd ed.
 1. Macroeconomics 2. Great Britain — Economic
 policy — 1945-
 I. Title
 330.941'0858   HC256.6

 ISBN 0-86003-053-9
 ISBN 0-86003-147-0 Pbk

Set by Typesetters (Birmingham) Limited
Printed by The Pitman Press, Bath

Contents

Preface vii

Part I Background

Introduction 3
  1 Textbook Models 8

Part II Factions

  2 Keynesians 27
  3 Monetarists 48
  4 New Classical Macroeconomics 66

Part III Issues

  5 Balance of Payments and Exchange Rates 87
  6 Inflation and Unemployment 107
  7 Crowding Out 129
  8 Business Cycles: Causes and Control 142
  9 Supply Shocks 158
  10 Macroeconomics in the 1980s 166

References 173

Index 179

Preface

The second edition of this book is considerably different from the first. The main changes are as follows. Chapters 2, 3 and 6 have been dropped. Chapter 10 has been almost entirely rewritten and forms the present Chapter 8. Chapters 2, 3, 5 and 6 are extended versions of the original chapters 4, 5, 7 and 8 respectively. Chapter 4 is new. Chapter 1 is little changed, as is Chapter 7 (originally 9). Chapter 9 is the old 11 with some changes. The new material increases the difficulty somewhat.

The last section of Chapter 2 is co-authored by Mono Chatterji and has benefited from a series of lectures given in May 1982 at Essex University by J. P. Benassy. The formalisation is due to him. The exposition is due to us. The new material in this edition has benefited from the comments of Mono Chatterji, Riccardo Faini and David Laidler. The Essex second-year undergraduates of 1982–3 have served as guinea pigs and seem to have survived.

K. A. Chrystal
Essex
April 1983

PART I
Background

The Introduction provides an explanation of the motivation of the book and some general comments on the new material added. Chapter 1 is intended to be revision for those who have already followed an introductory course in macroeconomics at the second-year undergraduate level. Those who have not followed such a course will find the treatment sparse at various points. Subsequent chapters refer back to the basic models. There are three main stages in the development of textbook models: first, the income-expenditure system; second, the IS-LM model which adds a monetary sector to the expenditure system; and third, the 'full' model which adds aggregate supply to the IS-LM model.

Introduction

This book is about two separate but related issues: one is the evolution of abstract thinking about the way a macroeconomy works; the other is the behaviour of the British economy. The British economy is used partly for purposes of illustration, but it is also of interest for its own sake. Some readers may find the balance between theory and description inappropriate – they are probably right. But bear in mind that the central purpose is to communicate ideas rather than to chronicle events.

With regard to the British economy, it will be seen that the major structural changes of the last decade are not easy to handle in any of the major analytical approaches. Policy proposals based upon traditional approaches should therefore be treated with caution. It is not obvious, for example, that so-called 'Monetarist' policies have been well conceived in the presence of these structural changes, but neither is it obvious that unemployment will be cured by massive Keynesian-style reflation. The problem is one of sectoral shift, not one of aggregate demand failure. Unemployment in the UK doubled between 1979 and 1983, despite the absence of any major fall in real domestic expenditure.

Macroeconomic Theory

The evolution of macroeconomic theory has been dominated by the so-called 'rational expectations revolution' (Begg 1982). This is associated with what has come to be known as the 'New Classical' school of economics. Much of the new material in this book is designed to introduce the student to this line of literature. The British economics profession is divided in its reaction to these new ideas. Many think it is erroneous and are waiting for the approach to die away. Some of the claims associated with this school are, indeed, outrageous. However, many of the insights which emerge from this line of reasoning are interesting and important. Macroeconomics will never be quite the same again.

One class of models popular within the New Classical paradigm considers actors with perfect foresight located in markets which clear continuously. There may be some benefit to be derived from conceptual experiments of this form, but they have nothing to say to the traditional problems of macroeconomics. There will be no discussion of this kind of model below. This does not mean that New Classical economics has nothing to offer in the way of understanding the short-term behaviour of an economy. The most interesting New Classical literature from a macroeconomic point of view is exactly that which posits actors in an uncertain environment with limited information, the nature of which is explicitly specified.

Rational expectations come in here when behaviour depends upon the expected value of any variable. The rational expectation is simply the optimal forecast, given the available information. This may not seem revolutionary, but it does have important implications for economic policy. An optimal forecast should incorporate *any* systematic information relevant to the variable being forecast. This may include the behaviour of policy makers themselves. Many New Classical models have the property that only unanticipated policy changes have real effects. This result depends not only upon rational expectations, but also upon the supply structure which is assumed. It will not necessarily be a property of all models with rational expectations. However, it does serve to illustrate the dangers of ignoring the endogeneity of policy makers.

One of the most important applications of rational expectations is to the understanding of exchange rate movements. Rudiger Dornbusch (1976b) has shown that, if the exchange rate adjusts faster than domestic prices, a change in monetary policy may then lead to exchange rate overshooting. Willem Buiter and Marcus Miller (1981a, 1981b) have developed this notion as an explanation for the over-appreciation of sterling in the 1979–82 period. It is argued below that this over-appreciation is causally related to the decline in manufacturing production and the resultant fall in manufacturing employment. However, the expansion of North Sea oil production is also emphasised as an important contributor to these events.

The area in which the New Classical economics is most vulnerable to criticism is with regard to the assumption of market clearing. Most New Classical models assume that prices adjust to clear markets continuously. This conflicts with the evidence that many prices are sticky and only adjust to excess demands or supplies with a lag. This is particularly relevant for labour markets. The New Classical insistence on equilibrium models makes it hard for them to explain such self-evident phenomena as unemployment and, in particular, its persistence. Surprisingly, perhaps, they are able to produce 'equilibrium' models which are consistent with the swings in activity characteristic of business cycles. For this, however, they need to rely on some form of rigidity other than sticky prices. The durability and irreversability of some investment decisions fulfil this role in tandem with lagged and imperfect information. Whether what is left is really a 'market clearing' model is a matter of semantics rather than economics. This is discussed in Chapter 8.

The New Classical economics is still too new to be fully assessed. However, its main value to date is that it is at least as much a methodological critique as it is a direct source of understanding of economic behaviour. The new macroeconomics is certainly more technically demanding, but it is yet to be proven as a guide to better economic policy. The general implication seems to point to the desirability of 'government' being small, stable and non-interventionist. However, one should be careful to distinguish implications from assumptions. Since the basic *assumption* is that markets do work, it should be no surprise to find that governments cannot improve the situation. The real issue for macroeconomics continues to be what it always was: in what ways does the market economy produce undesired outcomes, and can some government intervention improve the situation? Successive critiques by Monetarists and New Classicists have at least demonstrated that traditional Keynesian answers to these questions need refinement.

Economic Policy

At the time of writing, the two major political parties in Britain appear to be committed to extremist and radically different approaches to the solution of Britain's economic problem. The Conservative Party is sold on the free market approach that is labelled 'Political Monetarism' below. This has two separate strands of which one is 'Sound Money.' This can reasonably be associated with the term 'Monetarism.' The second is the idea that free enterprise will solve all ills if only it is given a chance. The public sector is seen as inefficient and obstructive and the taxes required to finance public services are seen as a disincentive to 'real' work. Wherever possible, activities are 'privatised' and an attempt is made to get 'Big Government off the backs of the People.' This second strand is really nineteenth-century *laissez-faire* economics in the best tradition of Adam Smith.

The 'Alternative Strategy' which is proposed by the Labour Party is based upon a very different view of the world. It is founded on a total disbelief in the benefits of the uncontrolled working of market forces. According to this view, salvation lies in a major expansion of state activity and state control. There should be a major increase in public expenditure, increased public ownership and participation in industry, restoration of external capital flow restrictions, withdrawal from the EEC and imposition of import controls.

It is not the purpose of this book to evaluate policy proposals such as these, though it is hard not to comment on the comparative role of wishful thinking and economic analysis in both strategies. The 'Lucas Critique' discussed in Chapter 4 below prepares one for the single obvious prediction which is that all radical changes in policy will have outcomes which are significantly different from those anticipated by their proponents – or, indeed, from those anticipated by any analyst at the time of inception. The popularity of the Social Democratic Party (SDP) before it had any policies may be significant.

The real purpose of what follows is to help the student to understand the major competing approaches to macroeconomics. This is interesting for its own sake – especially for those who have to pass an examination in the subject. More importantly, perhaps, it should contribute to an increased understanding of the environment in which we live. The reader will have to reach his/her own conclusions about the various policy approaches above (and *any* not yet manifest). This is not to say that what follows is a neutral and 'scientific' assessment. It is not – it is biased and selective. However, selectivity is not guided by the need to legitimise some preconceived policy recommendation. Rather, it is based upon either the pursuit of certain lines of reasoning which seem to be interesting or upon the implication of ideas which seem pertinent to 'relevant' events.

If there is any simple message, it is 'Be suspicious of economists bearing gifts.' Economics has a great deal to offer to the understanding of the economic policy problem, but a great disservice is done to us all by those who claim to have simple answers to what are, in reality, complex questions.

Plan of the Book

Chapter 1 contains a brief review of the core structures of typical macroeconomic models as will be found in virtually any textbook on the subject. An introduction to major schools of thought is provided in Chapters 2 to 4. Those distinguished are Keynesians, Monetarists and New Classicists. Coverage of the latter is the major innovation. Remaining chapters are devoted to a discussion of various issues. These are balance of payments and the exchange rate (Chapter 5), inflation and unemployment (Chapter 6), crowding out (Chapter 7), business cycles (Chapter 8) and supply shocks (Chapter 9). The final chapter draws together some dominant themes.

1

Textbook Models

The role of a model is to enable the economist to isolate the principal relationships between economic variables and to explore the logical consequences of changing these relationships. Textbook models start with a small number of simple relationships. Others are later added, in order to increase the realism of the model. How realistic any particular model is is largely a matter of judgement. The major controversies in macroeconomics are exactly about what constitutes a satisfactory model.

Most economists trained in the last twenty years will have been taught at least one of the models outlined below. When asked a question about the working of the economy, they will automatically structure their thought in terms of one of these models. The simple expenditure system and the IS-LM model should be familiar to all economists, though the full model with a supply side may be less so. These models provide a benchmark for the rest of the book. Of central concern throughout are the main channels of causation rather than the precise form of individual relationships.

Model I: The Expenditure System

This is the most familiar of all macro-models. It consists of an accounting identity and a number of equations determining various components of national expenditure. For the most part simple linear relationships will be presumed.

1.1 $\quad Y \equiv C + I + G + X - P$

National income, Y, is identically equal to consumption, C, plus investment, I, plus government expenditure, G, plus exports, X, minus imports, P.

1.2 $C = \alpha + \beta(Y - T)$

Consumption expenditure, C, depends upon disposable income (national income, Y, minus taxes, T).

1.3 $P = \gamma Y$

Imports, P, are proportional to national income, Y.

1.4 $X = X_0$

Exports, X, are exogenously determined.

1.5 $G = G_0$

Government expenditure, G, is exogenously determined.

1.6 $I = I_0$

Investment, I, is exogenously determined.

If tax revenue is also assumed to be fixed in size, the model is 'solved' by substituting equations 1.2–1.6 into 1.1, to yield:

1.7 $Y = \dfrac{\alpha + I_0 + G_0 + X_0 - \beta T}{1 - \beta + \gamma}$

This is the familiar 'multiplier' equation. The multiplier tells us how much national income changes in response to changes in exogenous expenditures. Its value depends upon the size of 'leakages' from the circular flow of income; notably, in this case, the marginal propensity to save, $1 - \beta$, and the marginal (and average) propensity to import, γ.

All the action in this model comes from changes in exogenous expenditures. It is presumed that there are unemployed resources so output is entirely demand-determined. Supply factors are passive and do not enter into the determination of national income. Thus the chain of causation in this model leads from exogenous expenditures through the multiplier to national income.

This simple framework is, however, sufficient to explain the essence of the so-called Keynesian revolution. National income could settle at an 'equilibrium' in the presence of unemployed resources. This would happen if exogenous expenditures were insufficient to generate the full employment level of output. The simple solution is that government expenditure should be used, in conjunction with taxes, to stimulate the economy in times of depression and 'deflate' the economy when it is 'overheated.' This, in a nutshell, is the intellectual basis of countercyclical budgetary policy.

Model I is encaptured diagrammatically in figure 1.1. The 45° line represents the accounting identity, or aggregate supply, since it represents points where domestic expenditure and output are equal.

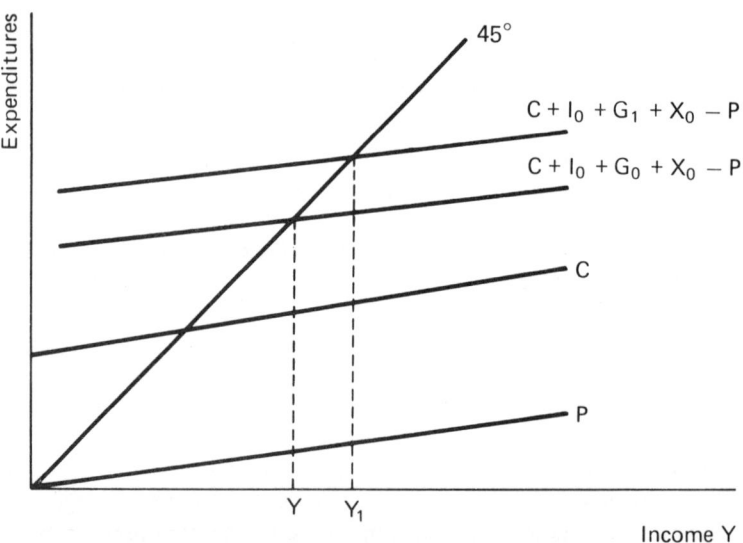

Figure 1.1   The expenditure system

The C and P lines represent the consumption and import functions respectively. Aggregate domestic demand is given by $C+I_0+X_0-P$. This determines an equilibrium level of national income (or output) Y. An increase of income and, therefore, of employment can be achieved by increasing government expenditure, G, to G_1. Aggregate demand thereby rises to $C+I_0+G_1+X_0-P$ and income rises to Y_1. Budgetary policy, that is changes in G and T, can thus be used to regulate the level of activity in the economy.

This is the first model learned by anyone who studies macroeconomics; it is, therefore, unnecessary to dwell upon it. However, a number of points should be made which will be referred to later. The first is that all the variables in the model are in 'real' terms, i.e. they are deflated by an appropriate price index. Thus inflation has no effect, since it shifts no relationship relative to another. It is common to talk of the existence of an 'inflationary gap' where aggregate expenditure exceeds aggregate output at full employment, but inflation would do nothing in this model to resolve such inconsistency.

Second, the model has nothing to say about the supply side of the economy. It is, in fact, presumed that resources are underemployed so that it is sufficient to look at *aggregate expenditure* in order to explain the determination of national output. National output is demand-determined. Obviously this has some relevance to deep depressions, but it is of questionable value in situations close to full employment. If expenditure exceeds output at 'full employment' the model becomes indeterminate. Finally, it is clear that if the workings of this economy are to be accurately predicted then the major intellectual effort has to go into the correct specification of the various expenditure functions, the consumption function being the most 'important' of these in terms of the proportion of total expenditure involved. It is a matter of some controversy whether the unemployment of the early 1980s can be cured by Keynesian-style reflation.

Model II: The Money Augmented Expenditure System: IS–LM

Model I was sufficient to explain the essence of the Keynesian revolution, but it was not the model of Keynes' *General Theory of Employment, Interest and Money*. One interpretation of this offered by Hicks (1937) included a stylised monetary sector. The monetary sector has two assets, money and bonds, the supply and demand for which determine 'the' interest rate, since the interest rate is the yield on bonds. Interest rate changes affect real expenditures through investment behaviour, which is presumed to be interest-sensitive. A reverse link from the expenditure sector to money arises because the demand for money for transactions purposes increases with the level of income. Thus equation 1.6 now becomes:

1.8 $\quad I = \delta - \epsilon r$

Investment is inversely related to the interest rate.

and in addition we have equations for the demand for and supply of money.

1.9 $\quad M_d = \zeta Y - \eta r$

Money demand increases with income and falls with the interest rate.

1.10 $\quad M_s = M_0$

Money supply is exogenously given.

The interest rate affects the demand for money because it is the opportunity cost of holding money. (Keynes' speculative demand depended on inelastic expectations but the model works in the same way.) There is no need to specify bond market equations because any financial wealth not held in money must be held in bonds. So demand for bonds is just the inverse of the demand for money. This assumption causes difficulty if we want to analyse changes in bond sales. It then becomes necessary to incorporate a wealth constraint explicitly.

The money market can be characterised as in figure 1.2 where the money demand line is drawn for a given Y. The M_d line traces the relation between r and money demand, or speculative demand. At higher levels of Y the M_d line shifts up because more money is demanded for transactions purposes. Thus for a given money supply higher levels of Y will be associated with higher levels of the interest rate, r. In the expenditure sector higher interest rates produce lower levels of income Y. This is because the increased interest rate reduces investment, which through the multiplier process reduces income.

Thus, we cannot solve the monetary sector or the expenditure sector separately since the outcome in each affects the other. The procedure adopted is to trace out two loci of combinations of

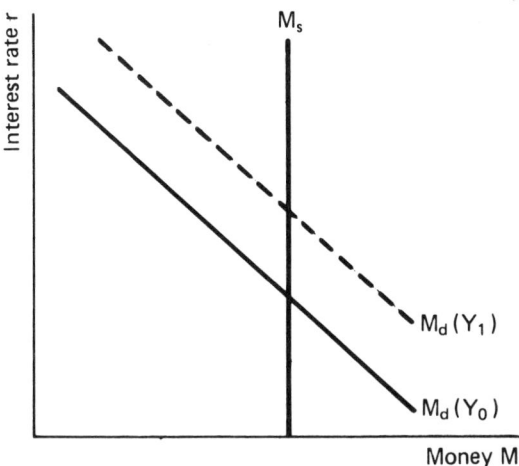

Figure 1.2 The money market

interest rates and income which are associated with equilibrium in each sector separately. Where these two lines cross, the values of Y and r so determined will be equilibrium values for the model as a whole. In figure 1.3 the line LM is made up of combinations of Y and r that are associated with equilibrium in the money market (i.e.

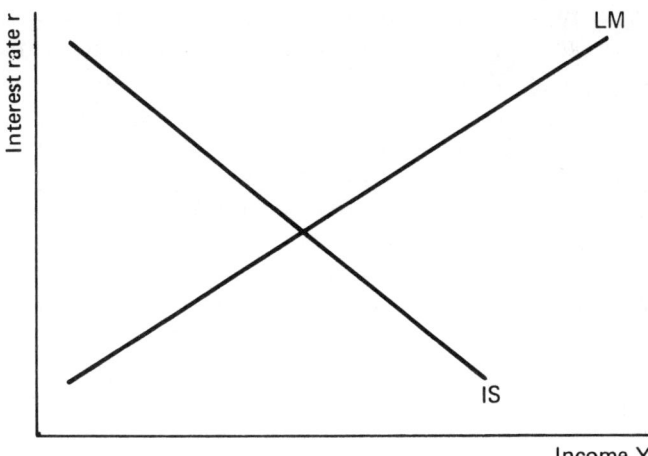

Figure 1.3

demand and supply of money are equal) and the line IS is made up of combinations of Y and r associated with equilibrium in the expenditure sector (i.e. injections equal withdrawals). The IS and LM curves are derived algebraically in the Appendix to this chapter.

This model still has variables determined in real terms. The money price level does not change, so changes in Y are changes in real output. It is, however, possible to allow changes in the price level but only at the expense of fixing real income Y, say at full employment. Then Y is no longer a variable and p is introduced in the money demand equation which now becomes:

1.11 $$\frac{M_d}{p} = \zeta \bar{Y} - \eta r$$

Real money demand depends upon the interest rate with income fixed.

The change arises because, whereas the money supply is nominal, money is demanded for its real purchasing power. Thus a rise in the price level reduces the *real* money supply. For a given real income the interest rate equating money demand and supply will be higher for a higher price level and for a given *nominal* money supply. To see this, re-label the horizontal axis in figure 1.2 M/p and shift the M_s line to the left. For a given M_s, M_s/p gets smaller as p rises.

The relevance of this modification to the model will appear below but it does illustrate one case of interest. If, when full-employment real output is fixed, the money supply is increased, the net result will be an increase in the price level proportional to the increase in M. This is the classical quantity theory result and it arises because all the real variables in the system are assumed to be fixed. As a result there can be only one real money stock, in equilibrium. An increase in the nominal money stock will be eroded by a rise in prices until the real money stock of the initial situation has been restored. However, this tells us nothing about the rate of inflation since we have a comparative static model not a dynamic one. We know that a once-and-for-all rise in the money supply will produce a once-and-for-all rise in the price level, but we cannot say what the time path of this adjustment will be.

Returning to the model where real income is variable and prices are fixed, it is worth noting how monetary factors influence real behaviour. A change in the money supply does not directly influence expenditures. Rather, it leads first of all to a readjustment of portfolios. An excess supply of money is an excess demand for bonds. This leads to a rise in the price of bonds, which is equivalent to a fall in the rate of interest, since the bonds are perpetuities. Only in so far as expenditures (of any kind) are interest-sensitive will there then be any real changes in response to the initial money supply increase. An important point is involved here since some researchers in the UK have found it difficult to pick up interest effects in the aggregate investment relationship (save for housing) and have thus concluded that money is of little importance. It is quite possible, however, that the link from money to expenditure is more direct. An excess money supply could be spent, not just on bonds, but also on goods.

If it were the case that an excess supply of money was spent directly on goods this would mean that evidence on the interest sensitivity of investment would not be important for judging the impact of money on the economy. Instead, we should expect to find terms in *excess* money balances appearing in expenditure equations such as the consumption function. It is difficult to incorporate asset stocks in expenditure functions short of specifying a full intertemporal optimisation model in which the time path of expenditures and assets are simultaneously chosen. The whole attraction of the IS-LM set up is exactly that the separability of expenditures and asset choices provides for welcome simplicity.

Model III: Aggregate Demand and Supply

The third commonly used model adds a supply side to the economy. Models I and II are essentially ways of explaining aggregate expenditures. The addition is now made of a productive sector within which the level of employment is determined as well as the level of real output. It is effectively assumed that the capital stock is fixed. There is, therefore, a production function relating output to the input of the variable factor (labour).

Labour is hired up to the point where the value of the marginal product of labour is equal to the wage rate, and the supply of labour is also assumed to depend upon the wage rate.

16 CONTROVERSIES IN MACROECONOMICS

1.12 $Y = f(K, L)$

Output is a function of capital and labour.

1.13 $L_d = \theta(w)$

Labour demand depends upon the wage rate.

1.14 $L_s = \lambda(w)$

Labour supply depends upon the wage rate.

The equilibrium in this sector can be illustrated with regard to labour demand and supply alone (see figure 1.4). Two important points need to be stressed. Firstly, increases in employment will be uniquely associated with increases in real national output and vice versa. This is because we have a given production function (1.12) in which labour is the only variable input. Secondly, we need to consider whether the labour demand and supply curves depend upon the money wage rate or upon the real wage rate, i.e. the money wage rate deflated by the price index of output.

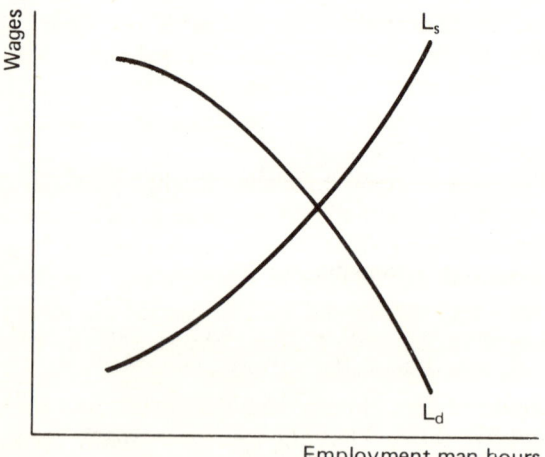

Figure 1.4

A moment's thought should make it clear that firms should only be interested in the real wage rate. If the price of output and the money wage rate increased together then the levels of real output and employment at which the money wage is equal to the value of the marginal product of labour will be unchanged. Thus it is reasonable to presume that the *demand* for labour depends upon the real wage. So far as the supply of labour is concerned it would be rational if this depended upon the real wage since leisure is effectively forfeited for *the goods that wages will buy*. However, it is sometimes assumed that workers do not fully appreciate or anticipate the extent to which money wage increases are offset by price increases. Accordingly, it is worth pursuing two alternative assumptions with regard to labour supply. The first is that labour supply depends upon the real wage and the second is that it depends upon the money wage or, equivalently, that workers offer labour based upon the *expected* price level and expectations lag behind the reality.

If both labour demand and supply depend upon the real wage then output and employment will be determined independently of nominal prices and wages. An increase in the price of output, accompanied by a rise in money wages, would have no real effect since the real wage would not change. However, if labour supply depended upon the money wage, an increase in money wages accompanied by a proportionate rise in prices would increase labour supply. In this case both prices and real output would rise. Workers would, in effect, be suffering from the *illusion* that their real wages had risen and would be acting *as if* labour supply depended upon the money wage.

It is now possible to derive what can be called aggregate demand and supply curves with both the price level *and* real income as endogenous variables. The aggregate supply curve is implicit in what has just been discussed. In the case in which labour supply depends upon the real wage, varying the price of output will leave the *real* value of output unchanged. Nothing concrete in the productive sector changes because all nominal values (i.e. prices expressed in terms of the numeraire, money) move together, and there is no change in relative prices. Here the aggregate supply curve, figure 1.5, is vertical since output is fixed independently of prices.

The situation is very different when labour supply is an increasing function of money wages, or workers act on price expectations which are incorrect. Now *any* rise in money wages is perceived as an increase in real wages so more labour is offered. If prices rise but money wages rise less fast, there will be an increase in labour supply

18 CONTROVERSIES IN MACROECONOMICS

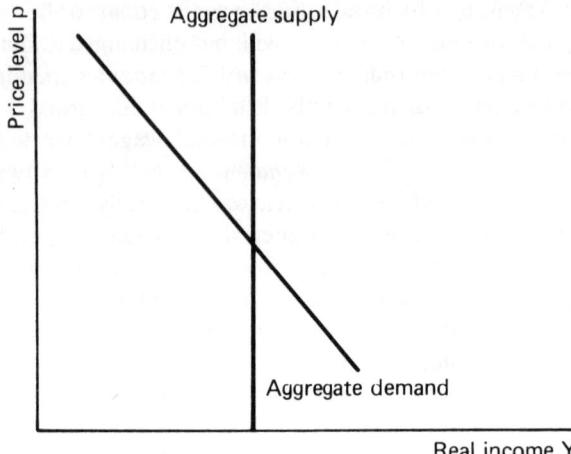

Figure 1.5

(money wage has risen) and at the same time an increase in quantity of labour demanded (real wage has fallen). Thus there will be an increase in employment and of real output. In short, on the assumption that there is some money illusion on the labour supply side, as prices rise there will be an increase in supply of output. The aggregate supply curve will be positively sloped. This version we call Model IIIA. Let the vertical aggregate supply be Model IIIB. The latter can be thought of as the long-run situation when workers come to anticipate the price level correctly. The former can be thought of as the short-run case when price rises are not fully anticipated. It is this distinction between anticipated and unanticipated changes in aggregate demand that is central to New Classical economics (see Chapter 4; for text which develops this approach, see Parkin and Bade 1982). Their conclusion that only unanticipated aggregate demand policy has real effects depends entirely on this distinction between Models IIIA and IIIB.

Derivation of the aggregate demand curve is entirely from the money augmented expenditure system Model II (see the Appendix to this chapter). It was noted earlier that Model II could be used to determine either real income or the price level but not both. However, it should now be noted that, for given values of all the exogenous variables (especially the nominal money supply), a higher price level will be associated with a lower level of real income. This is not because a higher price reduces the quantity demanded as in a single market demand situation. Rather, it is because, for a given nominal supply, a higher price level reduces the real money supply. As a result the LM curve shifts to the left, the interest rate rises and real expenditures fall. Real income, therefore, falls. Thus, the aggregate demand curve, drawn between the price level and real income, is negatively sloped, figure 1.5. Higher price levels are associated with lower levels of real income *when Model II is considered alone.*

A simple example will serve to illustrate how the full model works. Anything which in Model II would have shifted the IS curve to the right or the LM curve to the right will shift the aggregate demand curve to the right, i.e. an increase in exogenous expenditures or an increase in the money supply. Only an increase in the supply of factors of production or a technical change in the production will shift the aggregate supply curve to the right. Consider then an increase in exogenous investment in figure 1.6. The upper half of the diagram shows the IS and LM curves, the lower half shows the aggregate demand and supply curves.

The initial effect of an increase in investment is to shift the IS curve to the right, IS_0 to IS_1. In Model I, income would increase as a result of the simple multiplier to Y_3. In Model II the increase in income is less than this because the increase in income raises transactions demand for money and, therefore, bids up the interest rate. This increase in the interest rate reduces endogenous investment, which in turn reduces income. Thus in Model II income increases to $Y_2 (Y_2 < Y_3)$.

Y_2 would only be the outcome in Model III if the aggregate supply curve was horizontal, i.e. if all the output demanded were forthcoming at a fixed price level. It has been seen above that this is not likely. For the money illusion or short-run case there will be some increase in both the price level and real output. The aggregate supply curve in this case is S_A. National income will rise to Y_1. This is smaller again than Y_2. The reason for this is that the increase in the price level has reduced the *real* money supply so the LM curve has shifted to LM_1, thereby increasing the interest rate and reducing endogenous expenditures still further.

Where the aggregate supply curve is vertical, S_B (i.e. the long-run case where there is no money illusion on the labour supply side) there is no increase in real national income or output. It stays at Y_0.

20 CONTROVERSIES IN MACROECONOMICS

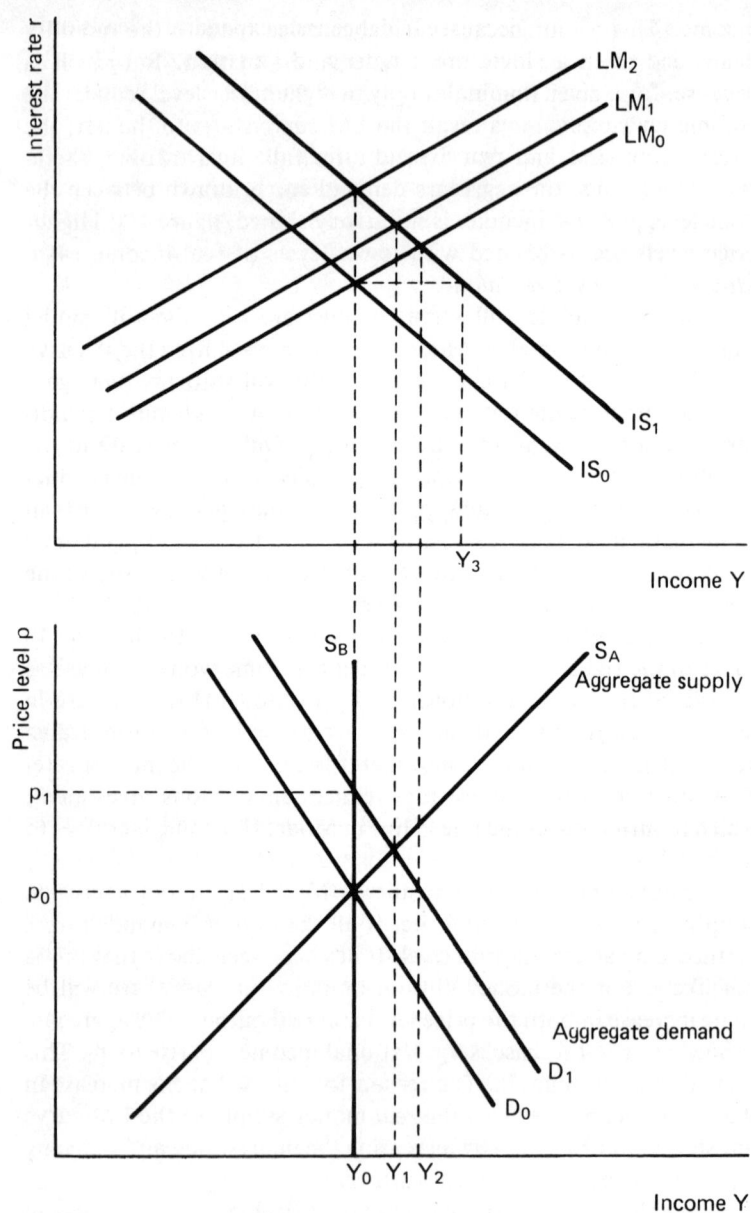

Figure 1.6 The full model

In this case, the initial increase in exogenous expenditure leads only to a rise in the price level, from p_0 to p_1. As a result the LM curve shifts to LM_2 such that its intersection with IS_1 is at exactly the original level of real income.

Each new model in this chapter represents an extension to the previous one. The above example shows clearly how the predictions change as we move from one model to another. For a given shift in exogenous variables, Model I predicts the greatest effect on real income, since *real* variables are the only ones to adjust. Model II reduces the real effects by adding an interest rate feedback. Model IIIA reduces the real effects still further by adding a price level feedback. Finally, in Model IIIB, real effects are entirely eliminated and the adjustment is entirely in terms of the price level, interest rates and other *nominal* values.

The term 'Keynesian' in macroeconomics is normally associated with Models I and II. Keynesians presume that increases in aggregate demand will produce significant increases in aggregate supply (except at full employment). Monetarists are associated with the position that, in the long run, increases in nominal aggregate demand will mainly be reflected in prices, with output tending to some 'natural' rate. The main difference between Monetarists and New Classicists is with respect to short-run dynamics. Monetarists believe that prices are sticky so that there are 'long and variable lags' in the adjustment process. A Monetarist would expect there to be temporary output changes in response to aggregate demand increases until prices have adjusted. In New Classical economics the price change is immediate if the aggregate demand change is anticipated. Model IIIA would thus be the Monetarist case during the adjustment period and it would be the New Classical case for unanticipated demand shocks. Model IIIB would be the long-run case for Monetarists and New Classicists and it would also be the short-run case for the latter when demand changes are anticipated. While New Classical economics assumes price flexibility, it is necessary to adduce other forms of stickiness in order to reconcile their models with real world data which exhibit obvious patterns of persistence. This point is expanded in Chapter 8.

Appendix

In this Appendix a derivation is offered of the IS and LM curves as

22 CONTROVERSIES IN MACROECONOMICS

well as of the aggregate demand curve. For simplicity we take a closed economy with no government sector. There are three equations for the aggregate expenditure sector and two for the monetary sector. These are given a simple linear form.

1a.1 $\quad Y = C + I$

1a.2 $\quad C = \alpha + \beta Y$

1a.3 $\quad I = \delta - \epsilon r$

These are the accounting identity, the consumption function and the investment function. Notation is standard and as in the chapter. The IS curve is derived by substituting for C and I into 1a.1. Thus

$$Y = \alpha + \beta Y + \delta - \epsilon r$$

$$Y - \beta Y = \alpha + \delta - \epsilon r$$

$$Y(1 - \beta) = \alpha + \delta - \epsilon r$$

1a.4 $\quad \boxed{Y = \dfrac{\alpha}{1-\beta} + \dfrac{\delta}{1-\beta} - \dfrac{\epsilon}{1-\beta} r}$

This is the IS curve. It shows a negative relationship between national income Y and the interest rate r. Notice also that an exogenous shift in consumption, α, or investment, δ, will shift the IS curve parallel to itself by the simple multiplier distance, $1/(1-\beta)$. The only difference that adding the government sector and foreign trade would make would be to add exogenous expenditures – government expenditure and exports – and the multiplier would become $1/[1-\beta(1-t)+\gamma]$, where t is the income tax rate and γ is the marginal propensity to import.

The monetary sector is very simple.

1a.5 $\quad M_s = \overline{M}$

1a.6 $\quad \dfrac{M_d}{p} = \zeta Y - \eta r$

Money supply, M_s, is exogenously determined by the authorities and demand for real money balances depends upon income and the rate of interest. Rewrite 1a.6 as

$$M_d = p(\zeta Y - \eta r)$$

Set money demand equal to money supply

$$\overline{M} = p(\zeta Y - \eta r)$$

1a.7
$$\boxed{Y = \frac{\overline{M}}{\zeta p} + \frac{\eta}{\zeta} r}$$

This is the LM curve. It expresses a positive relationship between Y and r, and it shifts as either the money stock M or the price level p changes. What we now have are two simultaneous equations in two unknowns Y and r. Notice that in 1a.7 the price level appears and is implicitly being held constant.

The aggregate demand curve tells us how changes in Y and p are related. Rearrange 1a.7 as an expression for r; substitute this into 1a.4. This gives

$$Y = \frac{\alpha}{1-\beta} + \frac{\delta}{1-\beta} - \frac{\epsilon \zeta Y}{(1-\beta)\eta} + \frac{\epsilon \overline{M}}{p\eta(1-\beta)}$$

The solution for Y is then

1a.8
$$\boxed{Y = \frac{\alpha}{(1-\beta) + \frac{\epsilon \zeta}{\eta}} + \frac{\delta}{(1-\beta) + \frac{\epsilon \zeta}{\eta}} + \frac{\epsilon \overline{M}}{p[\eta(1-\beta) + \epsilon \zeta]}}$$

This is the aggregate demand curve. A higher level of p will be associated with a lower level of equilibrium, Y. Notice that since this is essentially the 'solution' of the IS–LM system, the effect of exogenous expenditures on Y is now reduced because the 'multiplier' now includes feedback from the monetary sector $\epsilon\zeta/\eta$ as well as marginal expenditure leakages $(1-\beta)$.

The theory underlying the aggregate supply curve is discussed in Chapter 4.

Part II
Factions

Macroeconomics was originally Keynesian. Monetarists criticised the simple Keynesian view of the world. The Keynesian model was modified somewhat in response. While having something in common with Monetarists, the New Classical school regards traditional macroeconomics to have been on the wrong lines. The chapters in this Part are by way of introduction. Other important differences of view will emerge in later chapters.

2
Keynesians

Keynesian economics was what most people understood by 'macroeconomics' for the first two decades of the post Second World War period. By 1969, when President Nixon endorsed the famous dictum 'We are all Keynesians now', it was almost certainly no longer true. The Monetarist camp was sufficiently well established that the illusion of consensus could no longer be sustained. It might be tempting to suggest that the elections of Margaret Thatcher in the UK in 1979, and Ronald Reagan in the US in 1980, necessitate a revision of the dictum to 'We are all *Monetarists* now'. However, the big turnaround in policy stance, in the UK at least, came in 1976, not in 1979. The following quote, for example, refers to the Labour Government of James Callaghan:

> The extent of the retreat from the traditional Keynesian style of economic management, under this Government, could hardly have been made more clear than by the events of the past ten days. Minimum lending rate at 12½% and bank loans to top companies costing a record 5½% in real terms, combined with an officially expected slowdown in the economy, carries a very clear and simple message: the growth rate is now virtually the last thing the Chancellor takes into account when framing new policies. (Sunday Times, 19 November 1978, p. 63).

The purpose of this chapter is, first, to explain what is normally understood by 'the traditional Keynesian style of economic management' and, second, to provide a brief introduction to some recent developments in macroeconomics. These have come about as a result of attempts to re-interpret the economics of Keynes, as distinct from the model which was distilled from Keynes' writing by his early followers. It is the latter which we now refer to as 'Keynesian'. This interpretation was largely due to Hansen (1953), though it came to form the basis of the conventional wisdom in the UK.

The Keynesian Revolution and Keynesian Cases

The Keynesian model of how the economy works can either be thought of as Model I in its entirety or as special cases of Models II and III. It is convenient to discuss each of these in turn before discussing what the appellation 'Keynesian' normally means in policy discussions, though it is worth pointing out at the outset that the 'Keynesian' model was basically a closed economy model. This made its applicability to Britain doubtful from the start except in very special circumstances.

Consider the simplest possible version of Model I for an economy which has no imports or exports. There are just two equations – the national income accounting identity and the consumption function. Government expenditure and investment are exogenously given.

2.1 $\quad Y \equiv C + I + G$

2.2 $\quad C = \alpha + \beta Y$

2.3 $\quad G = G_0$

2.4 $\quad I = I_0$

All the variables are in real terms and all are *flows* of expenditure or income per period. It is presumed that there are unemployed resources, so that a change in the exogenous expenditures will produce an increase in real output and, therefore, of real income. The 'solution' to the model is obtained by substituting for C, G and I into 2.1 and solving for Y. Thus

2.5 $\quad Y = \dfrac{\alpha + I_0 + G_0}{1 - \beta}$

The coefficient on the exogenous expenditures, $1/(1-\beta)$, tells us how much income will change for any change in exogenous expenditures and is often known as 'the multiplier'. It is called this because if the coefficient β were to be of the order of 0.8, which is not unreasonable, then $1/(1-\beta)$ would be 5, i.e. a change in exogenous expenditures would produce a change in income five times greater.

The diagram used to explain Model I is familiar as figure 2.1. There is some level of national income at which all resources are fully employed, $\bar{Y}$. The principal message of the Keynesian revolution is that if aggregate expenditures are insufficient then the system will settle into an equilibrium (at least for a significant period) where resources are less than fully employed. The classical system, in contrast, was thought to work in such a way that prices adjusted up or down to clear all markets according to whether there was excess demand or supply. If investment and government expenditure are at levels $I_0 G_0$, then national income will be Y_0. At this level there is unemployment because the full employment level of national income is higher. There will be no tendency for this unemployment to disappear within the time horizon of the analysis. The major policy significance of this analysis, however, is that there is a simple solution to the problem.

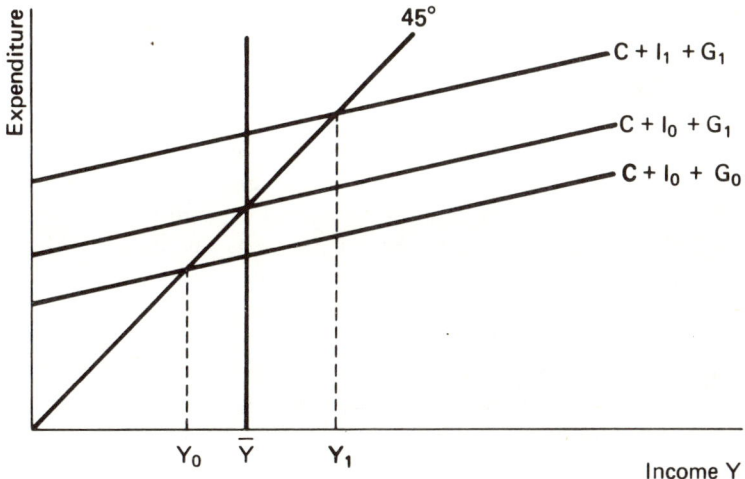

Figure 2.1

The cause of this unemployment is a deficiency of aggregate expenditures. It can be eliminated if the government is prepared to increase its net injection of expenditures into the system. This means that the government should deliberately spend more in the economy than it is raising in taxes. In other words, it should run a budget deficit. Previously, of course, the annual budget was simply a way of raising the right revenue to finance government expenditure. Keynesian economics is an intellectual justification for the use of the budget as the major tool for regulating the level of economic activity.

Model I is often referred to as the income–expenditure system or simply the expenditure system, as in Chapter 1. There can be no doubt at all that the formalisation of the analysis of effective demand failure which it presents was a fundamental breakthrough in economics. Economists of nearly all persuasions have added it to their analytical toolbox and would not question its relevance to the problem it was aimed at, i.e. deep and sustained depression. However, it would be foolish to claim that the apparatus is adequate to analyse other economic problems which have a different origin. For example, what if expenditures exceed full-employment real income at $C + I_1 + G_1$? Here it is common to refer to the existence of an inflationary gap (equal to $I_1 - I_0$). But inflation itself cannot remove this gap since all variables are in real terms. The model is incomplete. Macroeconomics today is still largely about what has been left out. Keynesians emphasise what was right with the model; Monetarists (and others) emphasise what was omitted.

The expenditure system is certainly not the model of Keynes' 'General Theory'. This is more usually, though perhaps incorrectly, interpreted as being the money-augmented expenditure system or IS–LM model. This is Model II of Chapter 1. The only additions are relationships for the demand and supply of money and a link from money interest rates to investment expenditures. The Keynesian message above can be shown in an exactly analogous way. Figure 2.2(a), for example, shows an equilibrium for the system at less than full-employment real income, $\bar{Y}$. Again the unemployment can be eliminated by an increase in the budget deficit, thus shifting the IS curve to the right. However, in that diagram the same result (with respect to income) could be achieved by increasing the money stock, thereby shifting LM to the right.

The numerical properties of Models I and II are not identical, however. It has already been seen that the multiplier is smaller in II than I because there is negative feedback from the monetary sector. Higher income increases demand for money which raises interest rates, for a given money stock. Keynesians have justified ignoring

KEYNESIANS 31

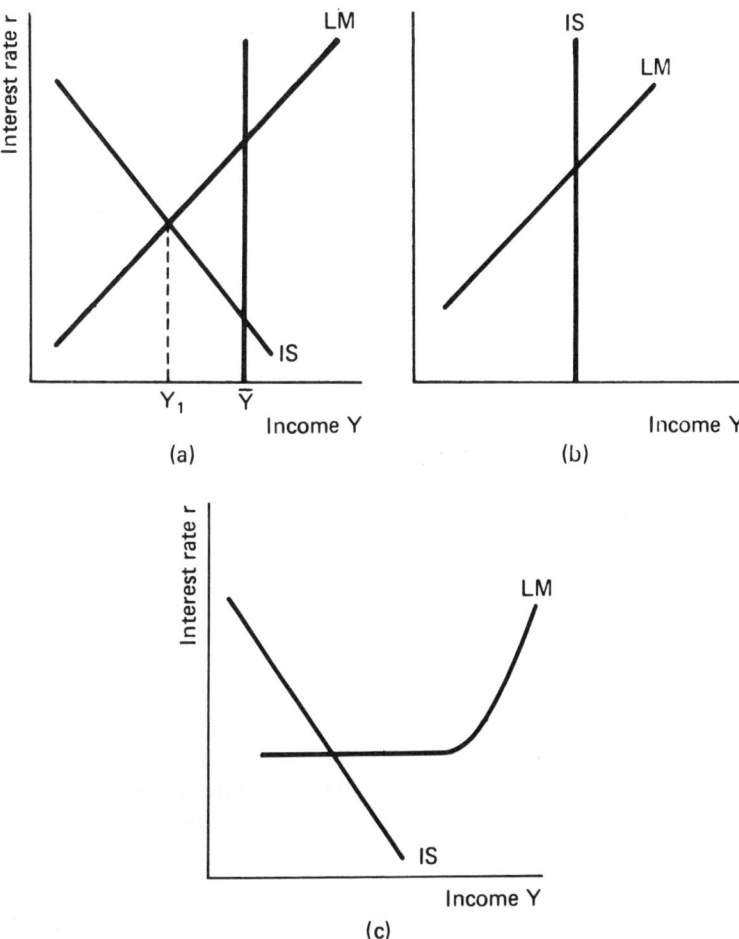

Figure 2.2

the monetary sector by the appropriate use of two specific assumptions, though neither is necessary to an understanding of the views of Keynes himself. Indeed, neither is contained in the 'General Theory'. The first of these is that investment is inelastic with respect to the rate of interest (figure 2.2(b)). If this were true, Model I could tell us all we need to know about the real economy. Money supply affects interest rates but interest rates do not affect any real behaviour. The simple multiplier is now appropriate. The second assumption is that there is a liquidity trap so that the LM curve is horizontal (figure 2.2(c)). This means that changes in the money stock get 'hoarded' and do not influence interest rates so there are no real effects even if investment is interest-elastic. This is the famous case of 'pushing on a string'.

While the latter assumption was used to justify Model I in its early days, British Keynesians increasingly defended their position, in the 1950s and 1960s, by reference to the former. The most influential empirical support for this view of investment behaviour was a survey of 37 businessmen reported by Meade and Andrews (1951), most of whom claimed that the interest rate did not influence their investment decisions. The same survey could in fact be used to sustain the opposite conclusion, since a small number of firms admitted that they were affected, which may amount to a significant effect in the aggregate. Nonetheless, it has to be admitted that at least until recently it has proved extremely difficult to establish an interest rate effect on investment in the UK, though this may be due more to the former policy of pegging interest rates than to investment behaviour itself. A survey of the evidence in this area is provided by Savage (1978) and a study which finds significant interest effects is Hines and Catephores (1970).

There is a special case of Model III which is often called Keynesian. Again it does not appear in Keynes' 'General Theory' but has entered popular discussion as if it did, following Modigliani (1944). This relies upon the assumption that, while there is no general money illusion, money wages are inflexible in a downward direction. If it is assumed that there is an initial equilibrium at full employment, then the aggregate supply curve is vertical above the equilibrium but sloped below the equilibrium, as in figure 2.3. In effect, the assumption of downward inflexibility of money wages means that there is money illusion in a downward but not an upward direction. A fall in aggregate demand from AD_0 to AD_1 produces a fall in prices. But, because money wages do not fall, the real wage rises. At a higher real wage firms employ less labour and, with a given capital stock, produce less output. So national income falls from $\bar{Y}$ to Y_1. Employment will remain at this new low level unless there is a reduction in money wages or an increase in aggregate demand. Above the full-employment level of output an increase in aggregate demand will increase the price level but not the level of real income. We shall see below that, while the case of real wages being too high is not essential for the existence of 'Keynesian' unemployment, it could form the basis of what is now known as 'classical' unemployment. Indeed, Keynes himself regarded it as the classical explanation of unemployment.

> Moreover, the contention that the unemployment which characterises a depression is due to a refusal by labour to accept a reduction of money-wages is not clearly supported by the facts. It is not very plausible to assert that unemployment in the United States in 1932 was due either to labour obstinately refusing to accept a reduction of money-wages or to its obstinately demanding a real wage beyond what the productivity of the economic machine was capable of furnishing . . . These facts from experience are a *prima facie* ground for questioning the adequacy of the classical analysis. (Keynes 1936, p. 9).

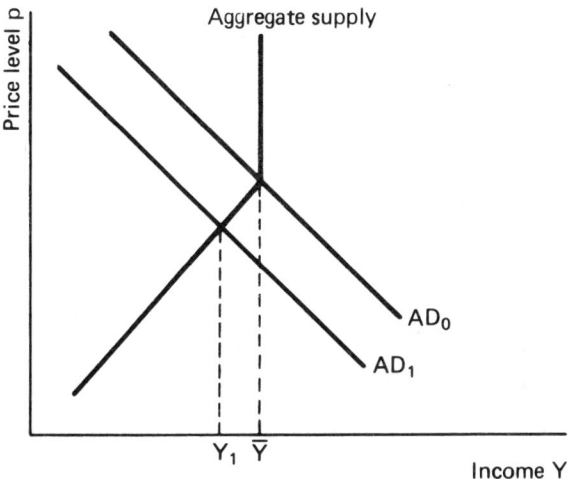

Figure 2.3

What Keynes clearly did believe, however, was that it is normally money wage rates that are specified in employment contracts so that, at least in the short run, money wages are more sticky than real wages. This was true for changes in either direction.

> Now ordinary experience tells us, beyond doubt, that a situation where labour stipulates (within limits) for a money-wage rather than a real wage, so far from being a mere possibility, is the normal case. (*op. cit*, p. 9).

If this were correct, the implications for aggregate supply would be quite straight-forward as we have seen in Chapter 1. The aggregate supply curve, such as that in figure 2.3, would simply be positively sloped throughout its length. A rise in AD would increase output because higher prices would be associated with *lower* real wages and an increased demand for labour. Higher money wages would increase labour supply.

Keynesian Economic Management

It is clear that macroeconomic management in the UK during the 1950s and 1960s was governed by Keynesian principles. The exchange rate was fixed, so the domestic inflation rate was clearly related to the world rate which was, in turn, very low. Economic policy was largely a tightrope walk with unemployment on one side and balance of payments deficits on the other. If the balance of payments was in crisis, as judged by the official reserves, the economy would be deflated. As a result, unemployment would rise, so reflation would be undertaken as soon as the reserve position seemed satisfactory. This pattern entered common parlance as the 'stop-go' cycle.

The economic instrument which adopted the centre of the stage was undoubtedly the budget, i.e. fiscal policy. Budgets were (and still are) normally annual events occurring in April, though it became quite commonplace to have 'mini budgets' in July or November. The experience of the time appeared to be that slightly excessive expansion ('overheating') would be associated with lower unemployment but slightly higher inflation and a deteriorating balance of payments. Overheating would be halted by a budget which raised taxes or reduced government expenditure. Slack would be taken up by the reverse.

Monetary policy was not non-existent, but it was largely a residual determined by either the necessity to finance the government borrowing requirement or by the imperatives of the external balance. The money stock was definitely not a target. If anything was a target it was the level of interest rates. In normal times the aim of the Bank of England would be to maintain an 'orderly market' for government debt. Any run on foreign exchange reserves would be countered, however, by a sharp upward rise in

Bank Rate, now known as Minimum Lending Rate. Monetary policy was thus constrained by the fiscal stance of the Treasury and by the commitment to a fixed exchange rate. It is now more fully realised how these two factors severely delimit the possibilities of independent monetary policy, particularly when international capital is highly mobile. Inconsistencies which arose in the 1960s were increasingly resolved by imposing quantitative ceilings on bank lending. These remained until they were swept away by the reforms known as 'Competition and Credit Control' which were introduced in September 1971.

This concentration upon fiscal policy probably explains why (in conjunction with the special assumptions mentioned above) the major forecasting models in the UK have been built largely as expenditure systems. Indeed, analysis which focuses upon expenditure changes leading through multipliers to income changes is the core of what most economists think of as Keynesian analysis. Later chapters will clarify 'the retreat' from Keynesian policies. However, a few points can be anticipated at this stage.

It is very important not to underestimate the importance of the external environment for an open economy like the UK. During the 1950s and early 1960s there was a steady growth in world trade and virtually no inflation in world prices. However, during the late 1960s world inflation began to accelerate, culminating in the commodity price boom and oil price rise in 1973. This has been attributed by some to US policies in financing the Vietnam War and by others to a series of coincidences. If the UK had retained a fairly restrictive policy during this period the economy would probably have benefited from export-led growth. However, the excessive domestic stimulation associated with the policies of Mr Barber, accompanied by currency depreciation, guaranteed that the internal inflationary experience would be worse than that abroad, as indeed the 1967 devaluation had led to a deterioration of domestic inflation.

The conventional (Keynesian) macroeconomic theory of the time had incorporated a Phillips curve (see Chapter 6) to explain inflation. This had inflation increasing as the pressure of demand increased. However, in the late 1960s and early 1970s there were periods of both rising inflation and rising unemployment. As inflation accelerated in the mid-1970s, with no obvious rise in the level of activity, the Monetarist criticisms of Keynesian economics began to gain credibility. Controlling the money supply became a dominant policy goal.

The Keynesian era is often characterised as a period when the authorities were most free to pursue discretionary fiscal policies. Nothing could be further from the truth. Whilst maintaining a fixed exchange rate, the authorities were heavily constrained. Any tendency to over-expansion would rapidly lead to a balance of payments crisis because of reserve losses. Money supply targets and self-imposed borrowing limits were unnecessary because such limits were implicit in the commitment to fix the exchange rate. Thus, it was not that there was no monetary policy in the 1950s and 1960s, it was just that the policy took a different form. Fixing the exchange rate, in fact, implies a far more severe monetary control mechanism than most alternatives.

Keynes Resurrected

(i) Introduction

It may be no coincidence that decline in the regard for the simple Keynesian model has been accompanied by a theoretical reappraisal of 'what Keynes really meant.' This has stimulated an upsurge in macroeconomic theory in what is now thought to be the tradition of Keynes. However, by splitting the Keynesians off from Keynes it has made them even more exposed to criticism than they were before. After the Reformation came the Inquisition.

The prime movers in the reappraisal of Keynes were Robert Clower (1965) and Axel Leijonhufvud (1968). Leijonhufvud's book was particularly important, partly in its own right but partly also because it explained to the economics profession some of the things Clower has been saying for some time. Leijonhufvud asks himself, 'How can it be that a deep depression associated with the greatest monetary collapse of all time leads to the story that money does not matter?' He concludes that:

> To the extent that preference for the use of fiscal measures for stabilisation purposes rests on the belief that they will have an amplified impact on aggregate demand, we do not find a case for them along the lines of analysis pursued here as far as states of the system 'fairly close' to full employment are concerned.

By pursuing Keynes' analysis we have ended up with an essentially 'monetary' view of Great Depressions. In a very general sense, at least, quantity theorists and Keynesians should be able to agree on one thing – how great disasters are fashioned. On one view or the other, the system becomes prone to them only when it has first been squeezed dry of 'liquidity'. (Leijonhufvud, 1969).

Here we offer a brief introduction to what is now known as the 'fix-price' literature. The following section provides a formal exposition.

The classical (Walrasian) model of a market economy was hypothesised to work by means of an imaginary 'auctioneer.' Transactors entered the market at the beginning of each 'week' with a set of goods and services on offer (supplies) and a set of demands which they would communicate to the auctioneer. There would then be an adjustment process (tatônnement), starting from some initial price vector, such that the prices of goods that were in excess demand would rise and the prices of goods in excess supply would fall. Trade would take place only when prices had been found which cleared the markets, i.e. equilibrium prices. In this way there could never be an excess supply in equilibrium (e.g. unemployment) because prices would adjust until it was eliminated. This is basically a barter economy since goods would now be exchanged for goods. Every offer of a good is simultaneously a demand for another, so Walras' Law (that the sum of excess demands and supplies is zero) must always hold.

One of Clower's contributions is to point out that in an actual monetary economy Walras' Law need not hold. Suppose an initial price vector exists such that some labour is unemployed. Workers have a supply of labour and a demand for goods. However, the demand for goods cannot be expressed in the market until after workers have received money for their labour. Firms are not going to hire labour until they see the money going down for the goods. It is Catch 22. The actual excess supply of labour is matched by a notional demand for goods, but, the *effective* demand for goods is deficient, so the workers do not get employed and the goods do not get produced.

What is shown here is that the existence of unemployment does not necessarily imply that the real wage is too high but rather that the whole price mechanism is at fault. False signals are being transmitted and there is no tendency for these signals to be quickly corrected. Prices themselves are relatively sticky so it is the quantities of employment and trade which have to suffer, but there is no presumption as to which prices are wrong so the mere reduction of money wages will not guarantee full employment.

The existence of money balances is vital to the behaviour of the system because they provide a buffer stock which insulates the economy against disturbances. Let us suppose that there is an exogenous fall in effective demand. Firms lose sales so they lay off workers. In Keynes' multiplier process the laid off workers cut spending, so more workers are laid off. The initial disturbance is amplified. However, this will only happen when the unemployed have been drained of their buffer stock of liquidity (i.e. in a depression following a monetary collapse). Otherwise the initially unemployed worker will, at least temporarily, maintain his effective demand by living off his buffer stock (his savings) and thereby cut the multiplier process short in its tracks – there will be no second round effect. Hence the conclusion of Leijonhufvud quoted above.

This reappraisal of Keynes has led in two related directions. First there is the temporary equilibrium literature which is beyond our scope to discuss, but second there is a rich and growing literature on constrained equilibrium macroeconomic models. The primary contributors to this literature have been Barro and Grossman (1976) and Malinvaud (1977).

		Goods market	
		Excess supply	Excess demand
Labour market	Excess supply	Keynesian unemployment	Classical unemployment
	Excess demand		Repressed inflation

Figure 2.4

Malinvaud develops a simple model in which there is a single goods market, a labour market and a stock of nominal money in existence. Nominal prices and wages are fixed. Analysis concerns the range of possible outcomes. There are two markets, each of which may show excess demand or supply, so there are four apparent cases. When suppliers are offering more than is demanded in both markets because of lack of effective demand, there is Keynesian unemployment (figure 2.4). If firms can sell all they produce but labour is unemployed, this is classical unemployment. The third case has excess demand in both markets, in which case, because prices are rigid, there is repressed inflation. The fourth case would have firms unable to sell all their output but at the same time demanding more labour than they can hire. This is ruled out as being inconsistent with rational behaviour on the part of firms, as they would not hire more workers if they could not sell even current output. So only three substantive cases remain.

These three areas of disequilibrium can be plotted in money

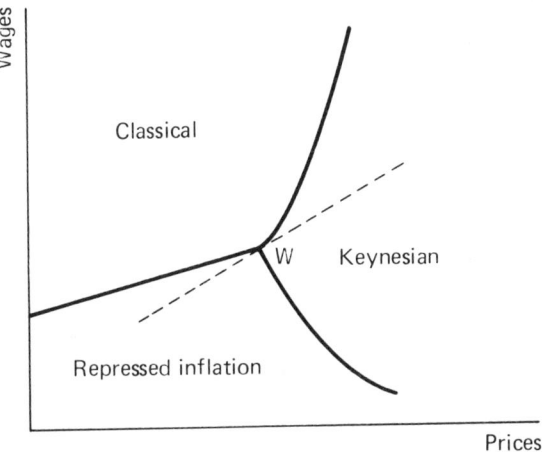

Figure 2.5

wage/money price space (figure 2.5). Recall that there is a given stock of nominal assets, M_0, and that whatever the prices happen to be they are not flexible. There is one combination of wages and prices which represents the Walrasian full-employment equilibrium, W.

> Roughly speaking, we may say that Keynesian unemployment occurs when prices are too high in comparison with the nominal assets M_0 of consumers and given the volume of autonomous demand g. Classical unemployment, on the other hand, is typical of a situation in which real wages are too high, so that firms do not find it profitable to employ all their labour force. Repressed inflation occurs when both prices and

wages are so low that individual assets have a large amount of purchasing power, and when people choose leisure to such an extent that the demand for goods, which may be high because of autonomous demand g, cannot be fully met. (Malinvaud, p. 85).

Malinvaud argues that the normal cyclical behaviour of the economy will be such that it moves between the Keynesian region and repressed inflation, as along the dotted line in figure 2.5. However, recent experience, partly explained by the terms of trade loss following the oil price rise, has included a significant dose of classical unemployment, i.e. excessive real wages. 'One may therefore understand why classical arguments about the causes of unemployment which fell into disrepute in the late forties are somewhat fashionable again.' (Malinvaud, p. 108). The next section derives regions, analogous to those above, in real wage-output space.

(ii) An Exposition

What the above discussion has shown is that there are really two characteristics which have to be highlighted in the identification of 'Keynesian' or 'Classical' unemployment. For Keynesian unemployment prices in general have to be 'too high', but there also has to be excess supply in both labour and product markets. For Classical unemployment the real wage is 'too high', but firms are not constrained in the product market. We will now present a formal exposition of these ideas.

There are two commodities – a physical good and labour – and one asset – money. Labour is the only factor used in the production of the good so its production function can be written

2.6 $\quad y = F(l)$

where y is the output per period and l is the labour input per period. The money prices of the good and labour are p and w respectively, so that w/p is the real wage. There is a fixed total labour supply l_o (though all of this may not be taken up). All profits from the firms are distributed to consumers (who are also the workers). Equilibrium output is denoted y^* and equilibrium employment is denoted l^*. Unemployment arises if l^* is less than l_o. In such circumstances it will also be true that $y^* < y_o$ where y_o is full-employment output ($y^* = F(l^*) < y_o = F(l_o)$). What, then, are the Classical and Keynesian explanations of l^* and y^*?

A Classical Unemployment

In the Classical theory firms are unconstrained so they maximise profit, given the real wage they face. They will hire labour up to the point where the marginal product of labour is equal to the real wage ($F'(l) = w/p$). This means that the Classical labour demand l_c is simply a function of the real wage ($l_c = (F')^{-1} w/p$). Output y_c will be whatever is produced by that amount of labour ($y_c = F(l_c) = F[(F')^{-1} w/p]$). If w/p is higher than is consistent with full employment then there will be unemployment ($l_c < l_o$). Notice that we are not explaining why the real wage is too high. We are merely pursuing the implication of it being too high for some unspecified reason. (This is one reason why many economists are critical of this method of procedure.)

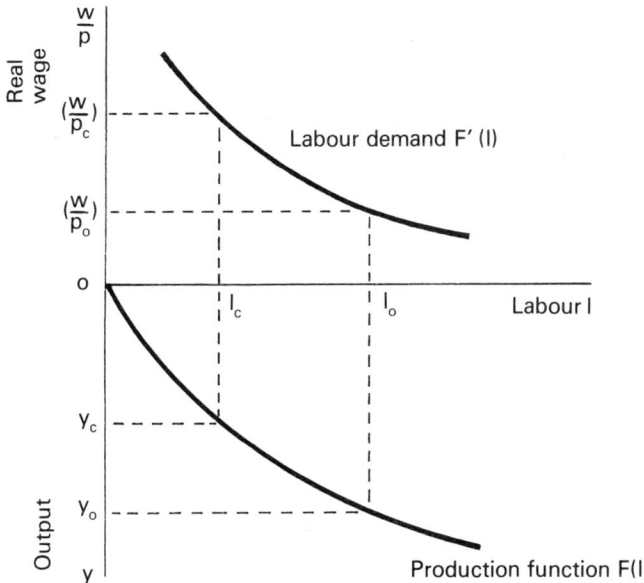

Figure 2.6

The Classical case is illustrated in figure 2.6. The upper half of the diagram plots the demand for labour at each real wage. The lower half plots the output produced by each quantity of labour. Full employment is at l_o with real wage (w/p_o) and output y_o. At some real wage (w/p_c) above (w/p_o) the demand for labour is reduced to l_c and the associated output is y_c.

B Keynesian Unemployment

The Keynesian approach is to start 'at the other end' by presuming that at the relevant set of prices (again chosen arbitrarily), firms are constrained by deficient aggregate demand. Aggregate demand is the sum of real consumption (c) and real government spending (g_o). Consumption is presumed to be an increasing function of disposable income $(y-t)$ and real money balance (M_o/p). The nominal money stock (M_o), the level of government spending and the level of taxes (t_o) are exogenously determined. There is, however, a balanced budget ($g_o = t_o$). Simultaneous changes in g and t will affect aggregate demand because the propensity to consume out of disposable income is less than unity. A balanced budget increase in g and t will raise aggregate demand. Equilibrium output y_k is determined, as in Model I in Chapter 1 above, by substituting the consumption function into the national income accounting identity.

2.7 $\quad y_k = c(y_k - t_o, \dfrac{M_o}{p}) + g_o$

This can be solved for y_k for any given values of t_o, M_o, p and g_o. Output will be greater, the greater is M_o and g_o and the smaller is p (t is assumed equal to g). This is exactly Model I except that investment is ignored (this is merely a simplifying assumption which can be included with no difficulty and, in reality, would have to be if there is to be non-zero saving) and consumption depends additionally on real money balances. Figure 2.7 illustrates the system.

At some value of taxes t, and government expenditure g, firms are sales constrained to produce output y_k. The labour required to produce y_k is l_k. At this output there is unemployment of $l_o - l_k$. An increase of g to g_o and t to t_o will generate full employment as would an appropriate rise in M or reduction of p. Indeed, this partial relationship between y and p for given values of M and g can be

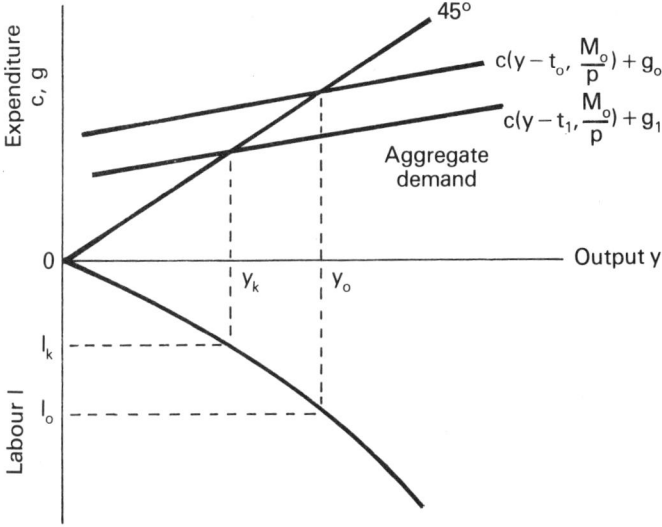

Figure 2.7

thought of as the aggregate demand curve of Model III in Chapter 1. Notice, however, that prices are strictly exogenous here and so we should draw p on the horizontal axis as in figure 2.8.

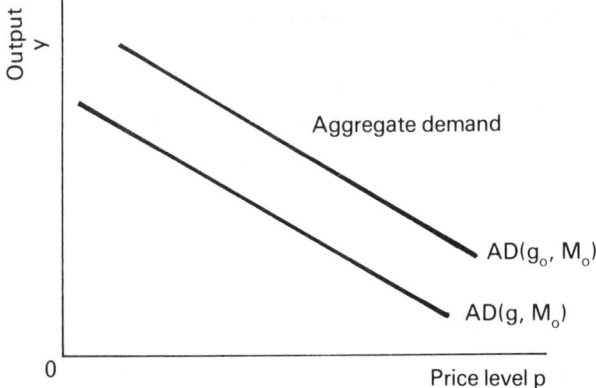

Figure 2.8

As above, g_0 is bigger than g. Any arbitrarily chosen p will be associated with some level of y given the other exogenous variables. So in the Keynesian framework unemployment is due to either too low g or M or too high a value of p. The real wage does not enter in at all because firms are constrained on their sales. Demand for labour is derived demand and so it will be inelastic with respect to real wages. Firms would not hire more at a lower real wage because they cannot sell any more output.

C Classification of Possibilities

We may now consider all the possible outcomes for all possible ranges of the exogenously given prices, wages, money stock and government expenditure. Two preliminaries are necessary before we can do this. Firstly, it should be clear that the constraint which is actually binding upon output will be the minimum of the Keynesian and Classical constraints. Firms will not hire up to the point where the marginal product of labour equals the real wage, if they are constrained on the sales side by deficient aggregate demand. Similarly, firms will not hire more labour at existing real wages, even in the presence of excess demand for the product, if they are already at their profit-maximising position. Secondly, output will also be constrained by full employment. So for some set of prices, g and M, there will be excess demand in all markets and no unemployment. This situation is referred to as 'repressed inflation'.

The equilibrium levels of output and employment, then, will be the minimum of the Keynesian, Classical and full-employment levels.

2.8 $\qquad y^* = \min (y_c, y_k, y_0)$

2.9 $\qquad l^* = \min (l_c(\frac{w}{p}), F^{-1}(y_k), l_0)$

Figure 2.9 can now be used to show the range of cases. There is nothing new in this picture, but it puts together the analysis we have already done. The south-east quadrant is simply the aggregate demand curve of figure 2.8 rotated 90° so that p now measures due south from the origin. The north-west quadrant contains a line ww which is a rectangular hyperbola. ww is drawn for a given money wage and it plots the resultant relationship between higher prices and lower real wages. The south-west quadrant contains a 45° line which ensures consistency between the price level which affects aggregate demand and the price level which affects real wages. The interesting construction now appears in the north-east quadrant. First note that there is one combination of output and the real wage at which there is full (Walrasian) market clearing. This point is w. To the south-east of w there will be an excess demand for both output and labour – recall that y_0 is the full employment output associated with l_0. If we raise the real wage above (w/p_0) we have seen that a Classical firm will choose to hire less labour and produce less. This was shown in figure 2.6. The line $y_c = F(w/p)$ in figure 2.9 simply plots this relationship between the real wage and output: $y_c = F[(F')^{-1}w/p]$. So, for example, at real wage (w/p_1), firms would be at point A with output y_1. Since y_1 is less than y_0 there would be unemployment of $l_0 - l_1$, where $y_1 = F(l_1)$.

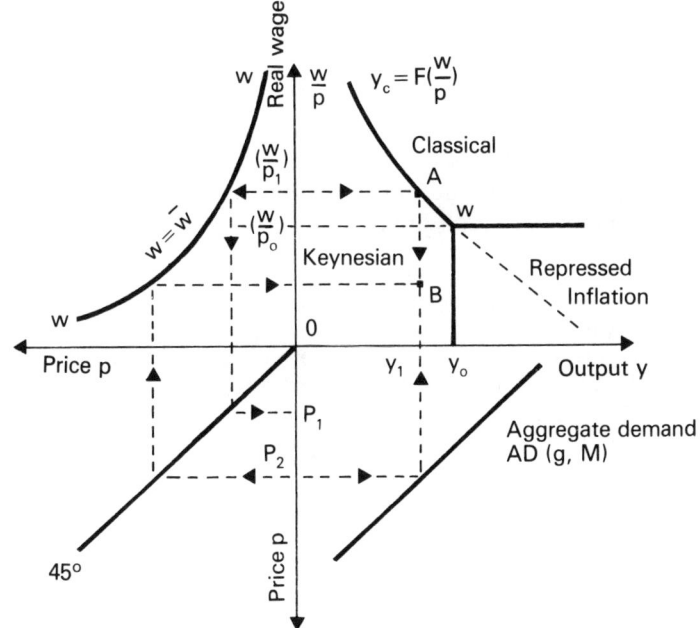

Figure 2.9

If the economy is to the left of the line made up of the vertical segment $y_o w$ and $y_c = F(w/p)$ then this must be because firms find themselves sales constrained. At a point like B, for example, the real wage is sufficiently low that Classical firms would hire all available labour. However, the aggregate demand constraint is binding so output is constrained to y_1 and, again, there is unemployment of $l_o - l_1$.

The way to use this diagram is as follows. For the Classical case set a real wage such as (w/p_1). Move east until the $y_c w y_o$ line is reached. This is the output level for that real wage. Moving west from (w/p_1) to ww and then south to p_1 merely determines the price level required for the money wage given by ww to give that real wage (w/p_1). For the Keynesian case start with a particular price level such as p_2. Move east and west from there to determine the intersection in the north-east quadrant, such as at B. If the intersection is not interior to the segment labelled Keynesian, then the demand constraint is not binding and one of the other two cases applies. Notice that points in the regions labelled Classical and 'repressed inflation' are merely *notional*. Points to the right of $y_c = F(w/p)$ would not be achieved because firms would not be maximising profit at that level of real wage. They will, therefore, rationally choose not to produce in that region[1]. Finally, notice that the position of w and the associated partitions are not in any way dependent on prices, money stock or exogenous expenditures. It is entirely determined by endowments, tastes and technology.

Three important implications can now be drawn from this analysis:

1. The key difference between Classical and Keynesian cases of unemployment is whether firms are sales constrained or not. Classical firms have no binding sales constraint; Keynesian firms do.
2. In the Classical case, lowering the real wage will reduce unemployment; in the Keynesian case it may not. To see that the latter is true, start at point B in figure 2.9. Now shift the ww line inwards.
3. In the Keynesian case an increase in aggregate demand will reduce unemployment, but whether it eliminates it entirely depends upon the real wage. If the real wage is above (w/p_o) an increase in aggregate demand will reduce unemployment, but only until the line $y_c = F(w/p)$ is reached. From then on there will be Classical unemployment *however high the level of aggregate demand*.

Finally, it is worth noting that Keynes' own view may be a special case of the above rather than the entire 'Keynesian' case. The question arises because Keynes talks about sticky money wages, but not about sticky prices. This raises the possibility that prices are determined endogenously. The only way this can happen in the above is if both the aggregate demand constraint *and* marginal product of labour constraint are just satisfied. Consider the money wage to be fixed whilst AD and $y_c = F(w/p)$ are as in figure 2.9. The price level is then uniquely determined as the only one consistent with the lines in all four quadrants. For unemployment to exist and for both constraints to be binding the economy must be on the boundary line ($y_c w$) between the Keynesian and Classical regions. Firms are profit maximising, prices are endogenous, but because money wages are fixed and the aggregate demand curve is fixed there may be unemployment.

Summary

Keynesian economics is about deficiencies of aggregate demand. The popular analysis of the issue offered the simple solution that the government budget could compensate for these deficiencies. Recent re-interpretations of Keynes have emphasised non-market clearing in the presence of sticky prices as the essential nature of Keynesian economics. The discrediting of pure Keynesian models has resulted from their inadequacy in inflationary periods. This inadequacy reflects the substantial neglect of supply side factors in the Keynesian approach.

Note

1 Firms may be on the boundary given by $y_c w y_o$ but they will not be in the interior of the Classical or Repressed Inflation areas. If they were in the interior of the Classical region they would not be maximising profits as the marginal product would not equal the real wage. They cannot be to the right of y_o because the maximum labour supply is l_o.

3
Monetarists

'Monetarism' is a term that is popularly used to describe an approach to macroeconomic policy whose principle characteristic is that it is non-Keynesian. In particular, it is widely used in the media in reference to the policies of political leaders such as Mrs Thatcher in Britain and President Reagan in the USA. Once a term becomes so widely used, of course, it ceases to have a very precise meaning. Nonetheless, it is important to try to understand what might be meant by 'Monetarism' in any particular context. A distinction will be drawn below between two rather different interpretations of the term. One has something to do with money and its role in the economy. The other, which will be called 'Political Monetarism', is little more than nineteenth-century *laissez-faire* economics.

Money in Static Models

It should be obvious that Model I has no room for a Monetarist interpretation since it has no explicit monetary sector or indeed assets of any kind. In Models II and III the cases which can be identified with Monetarism are often also called 'classical' cases.

The orthodox version of the classical case derives from what can be thought of as a special case of equation 1.9. This special case relates to what is commonly known as the quantity theory of money, though in classical economics it would be better called 'The Monetary Theory of the Price Level'. In modern economics it is part of the theory of the demand for real money balances. The quantity theory was based on an identity known as the equation of exchange.

3.1 $\quad MV \equiv pT$

where M is the number of units of money in circulation, V is the number of times per period each unit is used (velocity), p is the average price level per unit transaction, and T is the number of unit transactions per period. This merely says that the value of money paid out in transactions is equal to the value of goods sold. The theory is achieved by adding the assumptions that V and T are constant, or at least exogenous to the monetary sector. Hence, we have a theory that prices are proportional to the money stock (which in a gold standard model was exogenous).

The modern version of the quantity theory is not based on the turnover of money like the equation of exchange, but rather on the average money balances demanded to be held. The primogenitor of demand for money function is, ironically, known as the Cambridge Equation, since it was associated with such famous Cambridge economists as Pigou and Robertson. The Cambridge Equation says either that individuals hold nominal money balances in proportion to their nominal income or that they hold real money balances in proportion to their real income.

3.2 $\quad M = kYp$

3.3 $\quad \dfrac{M}{p} = kY$

where M is the money stock, Y is income, p is the price level, and k is a constant. By the late 1950s, however, when Friedman tried to provide empirical support in the US for a relationship similar to 3.3, this equation was no longer part of the apparatus of Cambridge economists. Indeed, it was complete anathema to most of them.

The only differences between equation 3.3 and equation 1.11 are, first, that here income is not presumed to be fixed at its full employment level and, second, the interest rate is missing here. The implications of this for the IS-LM diagram are straightforward. If we consider the fixed price level case, it is clear in figure 1.2 that, if the demand for money does not depend upon the rate of interest, the demand-for-money line is vertical. This means that for each level of the money supply there is only one level of income at which the demand and supply of money will be equal. The implications for the LM curve are shown in figure 3.1. The LM curve is vertical.

The policy implications of this case of the model should be obvious. Monetary policy means changing the money supply which shifts the LM curve. Fiscal policy shifts the IS curve. If income is the target variable it is clear that fiscal policy will have no effect on income, only on the interest rate. Monetary policy is the tool needed to control income. It is worth noting that, while textbooks often call this the classical case, it is far from classical in the fixed price level case. Only at full employment could figure 3.1 represent the classical case, and as a result monetary policy would only affect the price level and not real income.

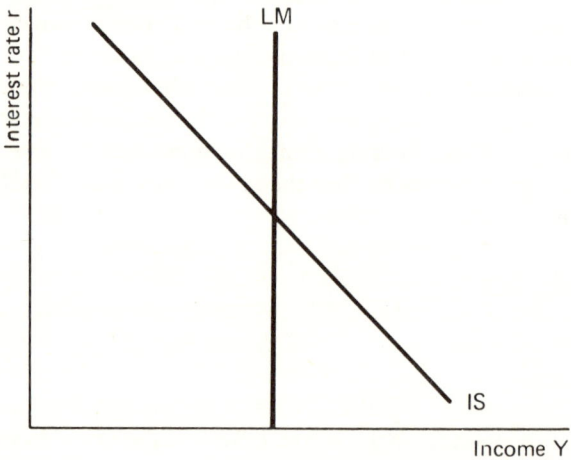

Figure 3.1

It must be emphasised immediately that not even extreme Monetarists would be likely to subscribe to the vertical LM theory today. Although Friedman in his early empirical work in the US claimed to have estimated a demand-for-money function in which the interest rate was insignificant, the vast bulk of work done since has found the interest rate to be important. So, while this case is of

MONETARISTS 51

historical interest, it need not be taken seriously as a practical possibility.

An alternative interpretation of the 'classical' case, and one which Monetarists may be more likely to subscribe to, can be thought of as being represented by Model IIIB. Here there is a supply side to the economy. Both labour supply and labour demand depend upon the *real* wage. This means that there is no change in aggregate output in response to shifts in aggregate demand. Changes in aggregate demand only affect the price level. This case is illustrated in figure 1.6 where S_B is the aggregate supply curve. A shift in aggregate demand from D_0 to D_1 will raise the price level from p_0 to p_1 but there will be no change in real income. This is actually a very significant piece of analysis and should be contrasted with the analysis in Model II, though it should be emphasised that even those who do subscribe to this view would regard it as a *long-run* case and not an accurate description of the short-run behaviour of the economy. We shall see in Chapter 6 how short-run behaviour is incorporated into this framework.

In Model II there seemed to be an important distinction between monetary and fiscal policy. However, in Model III monetary and fiscal policy can be seen as merely complementary aspects of aggregate demand policy. Aggregate demand policy itself is of limited use, especially in Model IIIB, because real output is not affected in the long run by shifts in aggregate demand. Only the price level changes. Thus, even in this simple static model there would seem to be little milage to be obtained from making a critical distinction between monetary and fiscal policy. This point is reinforced when it is realised that the possibilities for independent monetary and fiscal policies are severely limited anyway. The government's budget deficit (i.e. the difference between tax revenue and government expenditure) is, after all, almost identical to the public sector borrowing requirement (PSBR). The PSBR has to be financed either by borrowing from the Bank of England (printing money) or by sales of government debt. Both of these have implications for the money supply, so it would be very difficult to control the money supply if there was a large PSBR.

To summarise so far, monetary policy is of no importance in Model I. In Model II there is a clear difference between monetary and fiscal policy and whichever is the more powerful in controlling national income depends on the shapes of the IS and LM curves. In

Model IIIB real national output is independent of both monetary and fiscal policies in the aggregate. It is this last case which comes closest to the spirit of modern Monetarism, though there are many aspects of the latter which have still to be mentioned, especially with regard to the short-run behaviour of the economy.

Indeed, the major distinction between Monetarists and New Classical economics is precisely with respect to the short-run behaviour of the economy. The former would regard aggregate supply as responding to an increase in aggregate demand in the short run, whatever the nature of that demand increase; the latter claim that only 'unanticipated' changes in demand will have real effects. About the long run, there would be little disagreement.

The Real Balance Effect and The Transmission Mechanism

Important to an understanding of modern Monetarism is the story about how changes in the money supply are transmitted through the economy. The mechanism built into Models II and III is essentially the link proposed by Keynes which many would now see as insufficient. Basically, this relies upon changes in money stock first causing a portfolio disequilibrium. There is an excess money supply in portfolios and, therefore, excess demand for bonds. This leads to a rise in the price of bonds, which is equivalent to a fall in the rate of interest. The fall in the rate of interest then produces an increase in investment which through the multiplier effect influences income. As we have seen, much of the Keynesian disregard for monetary policy arose from the failure to find convincing evidence of a significant interest elasticity of investment expenditure. Many in the Monetarist camp, however, believe that the link from money to expenditure is much more direct. This direct link is often called the 'real balance effect'.

The earliest form of real balance effect was actually known as the Pigou Effect. This was usually applied to the behaviour of an economy in a depression when the price level was low. The effect arises because the low price level means that the real value of money balances is high. Consumers, in effect, make a capital gain on their money holdings and as a result spend more than they otherwise would for a given real income. The Pigou Effect was originally presented as an analytical device which would stabilise the macroeconomy, since it meant that prices would not fall indefinitely.

The real balance effect is more general than the Pigou Effect, though it relates to the same behavioural phenomenon. Anything which causes real money balances (or perhaps real liquid assets) to deviate from their desired level will cause a change in expenditures while the desired level of real balances is out of equilibrium. Thus a rise in the money supply could lead directly to an increase in expenditure. Instead of the excess money balances being reflected entirely as an excess demand for bonds, there would also be an excess demand for goods. The system as a whole cannot reduce its holdings of nominal money balances, so the excess real money balances have to be eliminated by either price level or real income increases until the nominal money supply is just demanded. Friedman has summarised this process as follows:

> If individuals as a whole were to try to reduce the number of dollars they held, they could not all do so, they would simply be playing a game of musical chairs. In trying to do so, however, they would raise the flow of expenditures and of money incomes since each would be trying to spend more than he receives; in the process adding to someone else's receipts, and, reciprocally, finding his own higher than anticipated because of the attempt by still others to spend more than they receive. In the process, prices would tend to rise, which would reduce the real value of cash balances, that is, the quantity of goods and services that the cash balances will buy.
>
> While individuals are thus frustrated in their attempt to reduce the number of dollars they hold, they succeed in achieving an equivalent change in their position, for the rise in money income and in prices reduces the ratio of these balances to their income and also the real value of these balances. The process will continue until this ratio and this real value are in accord with their desires. (M. Friedman, 1959, p. 609, Testimony in Hearings Before the Joint Economic Committee, Washington.)

There are considerable theoretical problems in specifying a real balance effect in a static macromodel, since it must of necessity be a disequilibrium phenomenon. The simplicity of the Keynesian model derives in large part from the separability of expenditures from the choice of financial assets. Indeed, Friedman's own permanent income theory of consumption implies that consumers' expenditure should be independent of asset composition. Nonetheless, several pieces of empirical work have purported to establish the existence of a real balance effect. Some models, such as Jonson

(1976), have this running from real money balances to consumption, whilst others tend to have causation running from 'liquid assets' to consumption. Thus Townend (1976) includes lagged liquid assets in his consumption function and the 1977 version of the UK Treasury forecasting model included a distributed lag for eleven quarters on 'gross liquid assets of the personal sector'.

Modern Monetarism

The focus of attention of modern Monetarism has moved on from the framework of the IS-LM model. There are a number of reasons for this, among which are (a) the lack of dynamics, (b) the absence of a supply side to the model, (c) the absence of a government budget constraint, and (d) the inappropriateness of the model to an open economy. The lack of dynamics is particularly crucial since it is now the rate of inflation rather than the price level which is judged to be important and expectations come to have a central role in behaviour. Consider, for example, the following statement by Laidler.

> An increase in the rate of expansion of the money supply to a pace faster than that necessary to validate an ongoing anticipated inflation will first lead to a buildup of real money balances, whose implicit own rate of return will therefore begin to fall relative to that on other assets. As a consequence, a process of substitution into all other assets and into current consumption will be set in motion, with interest rates, both observable and unobservable, falling. The ensuing increase in current production will set in motion a multiplier process . . .
>
> Along with the increase in output just postulated goes a tendency for firms to increase their prices and for money wages to rise to levels in excess of the values these variables were initially expected to take. Given that there initially exists an expected rate of inflation, this involves an acceleration of the actual inflation rate relative to that expected rate. If the actual rate influences the expected rate, the latter must also begin to rise. In its turn, an increase in the expected rate of inflation has two inter-related effects on variables involved in the transmission mechanism. It puts upward pressure on the rates of interest that assets denominated in nominal terms bear, and in increasing the opportunity cost of holding money, accentuates the very portfolio disequilibrium which sets going the first stage of the transmission mechanism and which accelerating inflation begins to offset. It also causes the inflation rate to accelerate further through its effect on price setting behaviour . . .
>
> Because . . . the expected and actual inflation rates will differ so long

as output is not at its 'natural' level, the new equilibrium, like the initial one, will see the economy operating at such a level of real output. The expected rate of inflation will be higher in this new equilibrium, and so the quantity of real balances held by the public will be smaller. *If* money is 'super-neutral'[1] so that the 'natural' output level is independent of the inflation rate, and of any past history of disequilibrium in the economy (both of these being dubious assumptions supported by no empirical evidence of which I am aware, and the former being contradicted by a good deal of theoretical argument), then we would also expect to find real rates of interest returning to their initial levels, with nominal rates having increased by the same amount as the inflation rate. If money is not 'superneutral' then we might find real rates either higher or lower in the new equilibrium. In either event, though, a higher and more rapidly rising volume of nominal expenditure would be associated with higher nominal interest rates. If real balances are to be lower in the new equilibrium, then, on average, during the transition towards it, the rate of inflation must exceed the rate of monetary expansion. Moreover, if nominal interest rates at first fall, but end up at a level higher than that ruling initially, they must on average rise during the transition. (Laidler (1978) pp. 170-1.)

This statement of the transmission mechanism may have been controversial in the early 1970s, but it would be considered 'mainstream' today. It raises several important issues which will be pursued in detail in later chapters. The most important of these are the 'natural rate' hypothesis, which is discussed in Chapter 6, and the implications for a floating exchange rate of 'a process of substitution into all other assets', including foreign assets (discussed in Chapter 5). Also important, of course, is the issue of 'expectations'. It is the hypothesis of 'rational expectations' in the presence of continuous market clearing that distinguishes 'New Classical' macroeconomics from Monetarism. Chapter 4 is largely concerned with this issue.

Demand for Money

It would be a misrepresentation of the Monetarist story to move on without saying something about the demand for money. One major tenet of the Monetarist tradition is that the demand for money is a stable function of a few variables. This contention was supported by a considerable amount of empirical work in the US in the late 1950s and the 1960s. A typical functional form for the relationship was:

3.4 $$\frac{M}{p} = \alpha Y^\beta r^\gamma$$

which, when all variables were transformed into logarithms, could be estimated as

3.5 $$\ln \frac{M}{p} = \alpha + \beta \ln Y + \gamma \ln r$$

where M is the nominal money stock, p is a price index, Y is real GDP and r is an interest rate on a substitute asset. One simple modification of this formulation involves the assumption that equation 3.4 is a desired demand level but that the actual holding is only partially adjusted towards this.

Little attention has traditionally been paid to the fact that both Y and r are endogenous variables. This means that estimation of equation 3.5 by ordinary least squares yields biased and inconsistent estimates of α, β and γ, owing to the existence of simultaneous equation bias. However, even more serious, as at least one interpretation of events indicates, is the question of identification. Whether or not equation 3.5 can be estimated correctly as it is depends upon what supply conditions are presumed to be. In principle, equation 3.5 alone could be a demand function, a supply function or some combination of the two. The assumption usually used to identify equation 3.5 as a demand function was that money supply was demand determined. Under fixed exchange rates, interest rates were primarily determined exogenously or with regard to the capital account of the balance of payments. To maintain interest rates at their target level, the authorities had to supply the money that was demanded.

It should be no surprise to learn that relationships such as equation 3.5 broke down in the early 1970s. This follows both a change in exchange rate policy and the change in domestic monetary policy known as Competition and Credit Control. (Indeed, several major macroeconomic relationships broke down in the 1970s, including the consumption function and the simple Phillips curve.) The breakdown was particularly bad when using M3, the broader definition of money, which includes interest-bearing time deposits as well as current account deposits. However, this is not surprising in the period when banks started to use interest rates to attract deposits. The mere fact that money demand equations which fitted well on earlier data broke down in the early 1970s should not be taken as evidence that such functions no longer exist. The truth may be simply that structural changes made the old estimation techniques inappropriate.

It has been shown by Artis and Lewis (1976) that a stable relationship can be fitted. They drop the assumption that the money stock is demand determined and substitute for it the assumption that supply is exogenous. The equation to be estimated is then an interest rate adjustment equation rather than a money demand equation. Its form is

3.6 $\quad \ln r = \alpha + \beta \ln Y + \gamma \ln M + \delta \ln r_{t-1}$

They show that this fits well for periods which include data from after 1971 as well as from before. However, it is worth noting that Hendry and Mizon (1978) present estimates of a demand for money function fitted to both pre- and post-1971 data. This has a more complex dynamic form than equation 3.5 and it appears to fit the data well, without making any allowances for structural change.

Finally, an important point about the interpretation of the 'short-run' demand for money function has been made by Laidler (1980, 1982). As has been stated above, it has been common practice to modify equations such as 3.5 above when estimated on short-run data (such as monthly or quarterly observations as opposed to annual, longer apart, or cycle averages). Such equations do not fit well unless some kind of slow adjustment is introduced. Common forms of partial adjustment mechanisms lead to the addition of a lagged dependent variable on the right-hand side of the regression equation. How is this adjustment to be interpreted in a closed economy or in a floating exchange rate economy where the nominal money supply is fixed and so cannot 'adjust' in any way? Laidler's answer is that what the short-run dynamics are really picking up is the adjustment of prices. As a result, what is being estimated is not really a short-run demand for money relationship, but rather a combination of the long-run demand for money function and a price-adjustment function. If this is true, it should be no surprise that the short-run demand for money has been unstable in a period when the behaviour of the price level has been so varied.

Money and Economic Policy

The perspective of money and its role in the economy has changed somewhat over time. It is important to realise that changing views about money are related to changing institutional structures which, indeed, imply a varying position for money and monetary control. It is, for example, no coincidence that the period in which Keynesians were able to relegate money to a passive and subsidiary role (at least in small open economies like Britain) was a period of fixed exchange rates and stable world prices. As we shall see in Chapter 5, a fixed exchange rate is a very rigid form of monetary control. Let us, then, consider briefly the changing view of the appropriate macroeconomic policy with special reference to monetary policy.

A hundred years ago there was no real macroeconomics. The economy as a whole was not seen to be something over which the Government had any control. Prices in markets were determined by forces of demand and supply. If there was an excess supply of anything, its price would adjust downwards until the market cleared. The only macroeconomic relationship that was widely accepted was the so-called 'Quantity Theory of Money'. Recall that, for the most part, we are talking about a world in which the amount of money in the economy was related more-or-less directly to the amount of gold in the country. Although paper money circulated, this was exchangeable into gold with the bank issuing the paper. This meant that the amount of paper currency banks were prepared to print was limited by the gold they held in their reserves. If there was an inflow of gold into the economy this meant that banks would be prepared to print more currency as they now had bigger reserves. Two important points should be emphasised. First, in the 'gold standard' system the supply of money in the economy was determined automatically by the combination of inflows from abroad and the behaviour of a large number of banks. The Government had no role at all in this story even for some time after the note issue was centralised.

Secondly, it was obvious to all observers that periods of inflation followed periods of gold inflows, i.e. rises in the money supply – hence the formulation of the Quantity Theory of Money. In its simplest form this says that the aggregate price index will be proportional to the money stock. This should not be objectionable

MONETARISTS 59

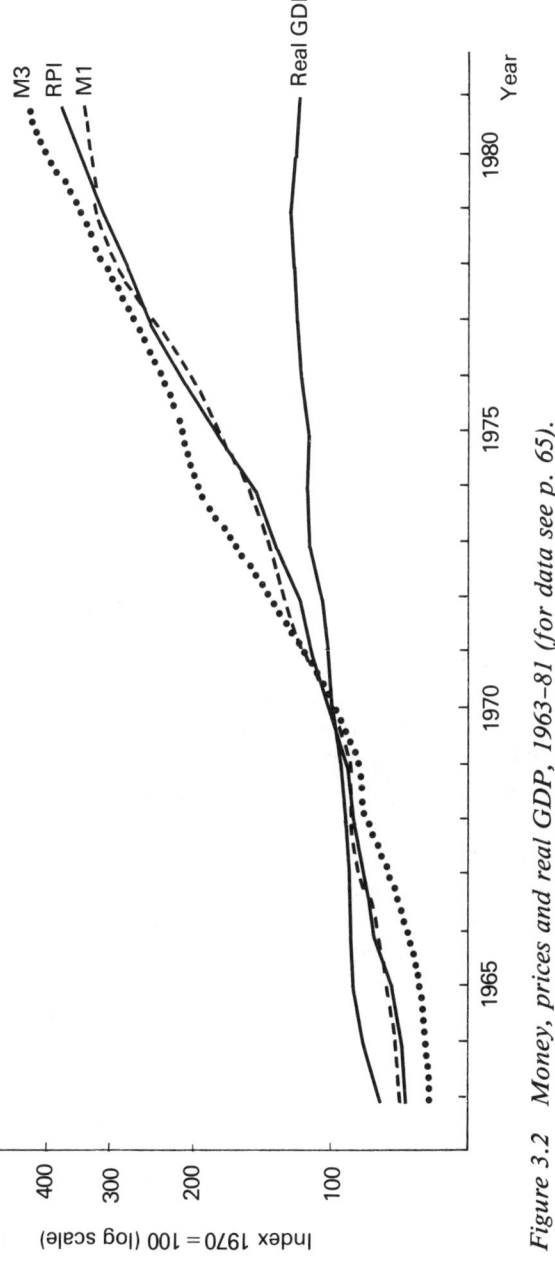

Figure 3.2 *Money, prices and real GDP, 1963–81 (for data see p. 65).*

since a 'price' is the number of units of money that exchange for a unit of a good. If there is twice as much money for the same volume of goods you would expect prices, on average, to double. The relationship between money and prices has continued to be a remarkably close one even in the recent past. Figure 3.2 shows index numbers (1970=100) for real GDP, two measures of the money stock (M1 and M3) and the retail price index, RPI. The close relationship between M1 and the RPI is nothing if not spectacular. However, no one would claim that causation is unidirectional as the data are drawn from periods of both fixed and floating exchange rates.

In the Classical system causation ran from money to aggregate prices, but money was not in the control of the Government. Relative prices adjusted in individual markets to equate demand and supply, so here again there was no role for government in general. What of the 'budget' in this world? The answer to this is very simple. Budgets were entirely an exercise in raising revenue to pay for the Government's expenditures. The guiding principle was the 'balanced budget' so that taxes were set to raise just enough money to pay for the Government's intended expenditures. Clearly something changed. What was it? There were, in fact, two major changes – one was structural and the other was intellectual.

The important structural change was the break from gold. This happened piecemeal, but was completed by the time the post Second World War domestic and international monetary system was established. In place of gold in the reserves of the banking system were the liabilities of the Treasury and the Bank of England. The fact could not be avoided that monetary policy was now a matter of central policy concern. For twenty years or so, however, monetary policy seemed to take a back seat to fiscal policy.

Fiscal policy, as we have seen, was the product of the Keynesian Revolution in economic thought. Monetary policy in the two decades after World War Two was largely passive. This arose from the commitment to fix the exchange rate. The connection may not seem obvious, but it is very important. If there was too much money circulating in Britain people would want to spend more abroad – either on goods or on investments. To spend abroad domestic residents had to buy foreign exchange. To stop the price of foreign exchange rising, the Bank of England had to buy the extra pounds offered *with dollars*. In other words, if too much money was generated the Bank had to buy it back with reserves of foreign exchange. Hence, even if too much money was 'printed' this would lead to a loss of reserves and a subsequent reversal of policy long before it has caused inflation of prices. In a sense, fixing the exchange rate *is* a rule for controlling the money supply and, in effect, ties domestic inflation to that in the world economy.

The only monetary problem that governments had was how to finance the budget deficits that fiscal policy required without leading directly to a loss of reserves. The problem arises from the fact that short-term government debt is a reserve asset for the banking system. So government borrowing from banks can lead directly to banks increasing the money supply. This is what is normally meant by the Government 'printing' money. Inconsistencies in this area of policy were met in the 1960s by the imposition of quantitative ceilings on bank lending which, in effect, swept the problem under the carpet by inhibiting the major clearing banks and stimulating the growth of uncontrolled secondary banks.

The groundwork for early Monetarism was laid by two separate areas of academic work, both contributed to by Milton Friedman. The first was the demonstration that the aggregate demand for money in the economy was a stable function of a few variables. This underlay the analysis which was offered on the effects of increasing the money supply. The rule of thumb was that a rise in the money stock would have a transitory effect on output after about a year and a permanent (upward) effect on prices after about two years. Other important ideas were developed in the context of the famous Phillips Curve (see Chapter 6). This had become widely accepted in the early 1960s as establishing that there was a stable trade-off between inflation and unemployment. If the Government were prepared to accept an increase of inflation it could achieve a reduction of unemployment. The revised theory, however, held that if unemployment was reduced below what Friedman called the 'natural' rate, this would not lead to stable inflation, but *ever accelerating* inflation.

The combined effect of these two developments was to reassert the validity of the Quantity Theory at least in the long run. Expanding the money stock could stimulate employment and output temporarily, but ultimately this effect would be reversed (or even more than reversed) and the only lasting effect would be a rise in prices in proportion to the rise in money stock. However, the relevance of these ideas was not generally appreciated in the UK in the late 1960s when they hit the academic community because, as we have seen, the money supply was effectively controlled by the commitment to pegging the exchange rate as well as by direct controls on the banks. Indeed, it is ironic to recall that after the election of 1970 an incoming Tory government inherited a balance of payments surplus, a budget surplus and a controlled money supply. The next three years changed all that in a way that was little short of disastrous.

Again, a structural change was integral to what followed. In fact, there were two important changes in 1971. The first was the floating of the dollar which was implied by the Nixon speech of 15 August. The second was the domestic reform known as Competition and Credit Control, introduced in September. This removed the direct controls on the banking system and had the effect of allowing the money supply, as measured by M3, to grow at a rate in the order of 25% per annum until the end of 1973 (see figure 3.2). It should be no surprise to find that inflation reached about 25% in 1975. The reason that this was now possible was that the pound was floating. Why did floating the pound have anything to do with it?

Monetary expansion with fixed exchange rates did not lead to inflation because, as we have seen, the Bank of England would buy back pounds with dollars to stop the exchange rate falling. Another way to think of this is that tying the value of our money to that of the dollar also ties our inflation rates together within limits. Monetary expansion with floating rates, however, is very different. Since the central bank does not buy back the pounds, people who find they have too many pounds spend them. If the economy as a whole is spending more than its income, this means there is a balance of payments deficit. The value of the pound *vis-à-vis* the dollar starts to fall. This leads directly to the sterling price of imports rising and prices in the shops soon follow. Under fixed exchange rates a monetary expansion leads directly to a reserve outflow. With floating exchange rates it leads to a depreciating currency and a build-up of domestic inflation as price rises feed through in wage rises and so on.

The expansionary monetary policy of 1971-3 was accompanied by a major fiscal stimulus following the March 1972 Budget of Mr Barber which set the course for the massive budget deficits of the late 1970s. There can be no serious doubts that the policies of the

1971-3 period were scandalously irresponsible and Britain has been suffering from them ever since. The central Monetarist proposition is substantially borne out by the evidence of this period, as figure 3.2 demonstrates. A massive monetary expansion led first to a short-lived boom followed by rapid inflation. This would have been true with or without the Oil Crisis which just made things a little worse.

Another irony of recent events is that the Labour Government of 1974-9 was the first to admit that the Monetarists were basically right. It was Mr Healey who introduced cash limits on Government expenditure as well as money supply targets. In this sense, at least, everybody has become Monetarist. Without fixed exchange rates or the gold standard, there has to be *some* method for controlling the money supply to avoid runaway inflation. There is still disagreement, however, even within the Monetarist camp, about how rigid monetary control needs to be. More importantly, perhaps, there is disagreement about how fast an ongoing inflation can be brought down by monetary control. Many, including Friedman himself, have argued for gradualism on the grounds that very tight monetary policy has severe real effects before it works to control prices. Others, such as Hayek, favour a 'short, sharp shock'. Those in the latter category would now be more likely to fall into the New Classical camp which will be discussed below.

These issues have, of course, assumed considerable importance in the UK as the rapid rise in unemployment since 1979 has almost universally been blamed upon Monetarism. This will also be discussed further below in the light of the analytical developments in Chapters 5 and 6. There is, however, rather more to the political and economic philosophy of leaders such as Mrs Thatcher and President Reagan than a desire to control the money supply. Since the whole package is often referred to as 'Monetarism', it is important to be clear that the rest of their approach is not related in any essential way to what has been described above as Monetarism.

Political Monetarism

The Monetarism that has been outlined above can be associated with statements such as 'There is a stable demand function for money' or 'Inflation is always and everywhere a monetary phenomenon'. It is possible to agree with these and yet be very far removed from what can now be called 'Political Monetarism'. Indeed, many Marxists would happily subscribe to at least the second of the above and many Communist countries have had tight monetary controls and low inflation (though the significance of this is less obvious in non-market economies). Clearly, there must be more to Political Monetarism.

Political Monetarism is closely related to nineteenth-century liberal *laissez-faire* economics. It is based on a belief in the benefits of the outcome of the working of free market forces, with government participation reduced to a minimum. It is true that many subscribe to both kinds of Monetarism, including Milton Friedman. This is, perhaps, the reason for confusion of terminology. However, this is the Friedman of *Capitalism and Freedom* and *Free to Choose*, rather than the Friedman of *Monetary History of the United States* and *Monetary Trends in the US and UK*. It is somewhat ironic that Friedman has consistently championed strict control of the banking industry and minimal regulation for almost everything else, when it is the banking industry to which he has devoted most of his scholarly attention.

Political Monetarism, then, is associated with a particular view about the role of government in the economy. It is the minimalist view – the 'get Big Government off the backs of the People' approach. Questions as to the appropriate role of government in a market economy and questions about monetary institutions and their control are quite separate. It is about the former that there is now the most controversy. (More will be said on this issue in Chapter 7.) However, the underlying theory of relevance is not traditionally regarded as part of macroeconomics. Accordingly, a full discussion goes beyond the scope of this book. An introduction to the main issues is available in Alt and Chrystal (1983, especially Chapter 1).

Summary

Monetarism, as the name implies, stresses the role of money in the economy. The link between money and inflation is particularly strong, especially in the long run, when the economy has fully adjusted. In the short run money can have real effects. But the presence of 'long and variable' lags makes the use of monetary policy as a control instrument inappropriate – hence the recommendation of rules for the control of monetary growth. The exchange rate regime makes a big difference to the way money should be viewed. With a fixed exchange rate the money stock is demand determined. Floating exchange rates make the money stock supply determined.

Appendix: Data for Figure 3.1

Year	M1	M3	Real GDP (1970 prices)	RPI
1963	76.5	65.0	82.1	73.9
1964	79.1	68.0	87.1	76.3
1965	80.8	73.0	89.3	80.0
1966	80.7	75.5	91.1	83.1
1967	86.8	83.0	93.4	85.2
1968	91.7	89.5	96.8	89.2
1969	91.9	91.4	98.2	94.0
1970	100.0	100.0	100.0	100.0
1971	113.7	112.9	102.2	109.4
1972	130.1	143.5	103.9	117.6
1973	136.9	180.0	109.4	128.0
1974	152.0	200.0	110.5	148.5
1975	181.0	213.4	109.7	184.5
1976	201.5	233.4	113.76	214.9
1977	246.0	256.9	115.3	249.1
1978	287.0	296.5	118.9	270.0
1979	319.0	334.0	120.6	304.8
1980	324.0	396.7	118.0	361.0
1981	356.0	451.0	115.4	404.0

Index Numbers of Money Stock, Real GDP and Retail Price Index (RPI) 1970 = 100
Source: Derived from Economic Trends.

4
New Classical Macroeconomics

The bulk of attention in the last decade has been directed, within the macroeconomics literature, to the work of the New Classical School of economists. The terminology is not universally accepted since some prefer to call them Neo-Austrians. However, what is important is to make a clear distinction between this group and Monetarists. It is certainly true that New Classical ideas evolved out of Monetarism and that many former Monetarists have travelled on. What is not true is that it is safe to subsume one set of ideas within the other set.

The distinguishing feature of New Classical (NC) economics is often said to be the 'rational expectations hypothesis'. This is indeed important, but it is now clear that three other assumptions also play an important role in the typical NC analysis. These are the assumption of clearing markets, the natural rate hypothesis and the nature of the aggregate supply curve. Logically, these three are really only two independent assumptions (i.e. what is the supply curve, and is the economy always on both demand and supply curves?). However, they are stated this way for ease of recognition. The natural rate hypothesis in its stronger version requires both long-run market clearing and a specific supply structure to the economy.

The New Classical School is posing such a major challenge to conventional macroeconomics that the latter cannot survive unchanged. However, much of the New Classical literature is technically demanding so that it is hard for practitioners to read, let alone the typical undergraduate. As a result, it may be some time before their ideas are fully assimilated and assessed.

The Main Drift

For the NC economist the economy is made up of actors who consistently pursue the maximisation of some clearly-defined objective function. The actors trade with one another in well-organised markets. Trade takes place at market clearing prices such that all who wish to trade at the going prices are able to do so. This far, the framework would be recognised by any Classical economist. Novelty arises from the fact that the NC economist will not locate these actors in a static world, but rather in a stochastic environment. The world is one in which there are *recurrent shocks* to the system – bad harvests, earthquakes, sunspots, policy shifts, exogenous taste changes, wars etc. In other words, while actors are rationally trying to respond to the price signals of the market, these signals are 'noisy'. The fact that they are noisy has important implications. The NC world is often characterised as being 'perfect' in the sense of full information and costless adjustment. Some NC models are like this, but these are not the interesting ones. It is central to the NC explanations of macroeconomic fluctuations that information is incomplete and that some adjustments are costly – that is, prior commitments are recurrently made.

An individual does not wait to find out the complete set of prices and then make all his supply/demand decisions at those actual prices (as he might do in the presence of a Walrasian auctioneer). Rather, some decisions have to be made before the price which would affect it has actually been determined. For example, a wage contract may be entered into before work begins and a factory must be built before it can produce. These commitments must be made on the basis of the *expectations* of what the relevant prices will be. But it is to be emphasised that these expectations can, and will in general, be incorrect because the actual outcome is affected by current disturbances.

The rational expectations hypothesis simply amounts to the assumption that, in forming their expectations of what these prices (and perhaps other variables) will be, actors *do the best that they can*. This means that, given the information available at the time the forecast is made, no better forecast could be made on the basis of the same information. This does not imply either that the rational forecast will be correct or that some other guess would not be better for specific episodes. What it does imply is that a 'rational' forecast will, *on average*, be correct and that no other forecasting technique will regularly beat it. If the rational forecast was not correct on average, such systematic error would imply that information was not being fully utilised. This would contradict the notion of rationality. Equally, if there was a way of making forecasts better on average, that information should be included in the rational forecast.

The notion of rational expectations should not be alien to economists. Indeed, since the rational forecast is *defined* as optimal it is hard to support any other. To define the optimal forecast, of course, does not commit us to the view that all actors *actually do* forecast optimally all the time, any more than to define profit maximisation commits us to the view that all firms maximise profits continuously. What it does do is enable us to examine the logical implications of rational forecasts as well as of deviations from full rationality. The New Classical economics has been mistakenly criticised for its use of rational expectations on the grounds that it requires that actors know too much, or more than they can reasonably be expected to know. It is true that some of the literature requires actors to know all that there is to know. However, much of the NC literature achieves its milage precisely by restricting the information available to actors at the time they make their decisions. Lucas (1973) is a good example of this, where actors are presumed to know current prices in the market in which they sell their product, but only to learn about the general price level with a lag.

This far the discussion may seem to have been unnecessarily abstract. These abstract ideas do, however, have powerful implications for the way we view macroeconomic policy. It is these implications which have attracted so much attention to the NC economics. Most famous is the result that systematic aggregate demand policies can have no real effect. Recall that Keynesian economics was invented to show ways in which governments could raise the level of activity in the economy. An argument which says that policy can have no effect will obviously be a spark to considerable controversy. The argument will simply be stated here and discussed further below.

Consider an economy which is at full employment in the sense that the labour market clears at a given real wage. The capital stock is held constant. We know that if all prices and incomes double in nominal terms nothing real will change. Suppose the authorities announce that the money stock is about to double. Rational actors would double their prices and so there would be no real effect. However, if the authorities doubled the money stock without telling anyone they were going to do it, firms and workers may think that there is an increased real demand for their services and so increase their supply. Hence, the short-term effect on the economy will depend crucially upon whether the policy change was anticipated or unanticipated. Only unanticipated aggregate demand policies will have real effects.

A useful way to think of the difference between Keynesian and New Classical perceptions of policy is to notice that a Keynesian would consider the policy maker to be exogenous to the economy, and so all policies would be unanticipated. In the new view, however, to the extent that the policy maker responds systematically to the state of the economy, actors learn that this is what they will do and change their own behaviour accordingly. More fundamentally, perhaps, it means that the behaviour of the economy will differ with each policy regime. Let us now look at this in more detail.

The New Classical Challenge

It has been argued above that Monetarism could be viewed as an evolutionary stage in macroeconomics which started with the simple Keynesian model. While clearly emerging from a Monetarist background, New Classical macroeconomics represents a clean break from the stance of Keynesian economics. The nature of this break is nowhere more clearly evident than in a paper by Robert Lucas and Thomas Sargent (1981a) entitled *After Keynesian Macroeconomics*:

> For the applied economist, the confident and apparently successful application of Keynesian principles to economic policy which occurred in the United States in the 1960s was an event of incomparable significance and satisfaction. These principles led to a set of simple, quantitative relationships between fiscal policy and economic activity generally, the basic logic of which could be (and was) explained to the general public and which could be applied to yield improvements in economic performance benefiting everyone. . . We dwell on these halcyon days of Keynesian economics because without conscious effort they are difficult to recall today. In the present decade, the US economy has

undergone its first major depression since the 1930s to the accompaniment of inflation rates in excess of 10 per cent per annum. These events have been transmitted (by consent of the governments involved) to other advanced countries and in many cases have been amplified. The events did not arise from a reactionary reversion to outmoded, 'classical' principles of tight money and balanced budgets. On the contrary, they were accompanied by massive government budget deficits and high rates of monetary expansion, policies which, although bearing an admitted risk of inflation, promised according to modern Keynesian doctrine rapid real growth and low rates of unemployment.

That these predictions were wildly incorrect and that the doctrine on which they were based is fundamentally flawed are now simple matters of fact, involving no novelties in economic theory. The task now facing contemporary students of the business cycle is to sort through the wreckage, determining which feature of that remarkable intellectual event called the Keynesian Revolution can be salvaged and put to good use and which others must be discarded ... Our intention is to establish that the difficulties are *fatal*, that modern macroeconomic models are of *no* value in guiding policy and that this condition will not be remedied by modifications along any line which is currently being pursued. (Lucas and Sargent (eds) 1981a, pp. 295-313)

What is the basis for such strong claims about Keynesian macroeconomics? The argument is now known as the Lucas Critique after the title of the famous paper in which the argument first appeared ('Econometric policy evaluation: a critique', Lucas 1976). It should be emphasised in advance that these criticisms do not depend in any essential way on the assumptions typically used by the New Classical economists themselves. In other words, it is possible to accept the criticisms without in any way accepting the New Classical view of the appropriate solutions. Before explaining the criticisms, of course, it is necessary to have some idea of what Keynesian methodology was supposed to have been.

Consider the simple expenditure system given by equations 1.1 to 1.6 in Chapter 1. A real model used for policy analysis would be more complicated than this, but the point can be made just as well in this stripped-down version. Let us just take the 'multiplier' equation 1.7:

$$Y = \frac{\alpha + I_o + G_o + X_o - \beta T}{1 - \beta + \gamma}$$

The Keynesian strategy would be straightforward. First, estimate the parameters α, β and γ from available historical data. Form some view of the likely values of the exogenous variables I_o and X_o. Forecast the value of Y on the basis of the estimated parameters and the predicted values of the exogenous variables, assuming that the policy instruments G_o and T are unchanged. Then see what would happen to Y under different assumptions about values of the policy instruments. Choose values of the policy instruments which generate the most desirable outcome by some criterion.

The Lucas criticism is that, while it may produce reasonable short-term forecasts, it is not an appropriate tool for the analysis of alternative policy scenarios. The short-term forecasts are reasonable because actual forecasting models incorporate lots of lagged variables. So forecasting just amounts to an extrapolation of what is going on already. Policy analysis, however, is worthless because the estimated parameters α, β, γ etc will not be invariant to the policies chosen. Even the assumed values of the 'exogenous' variables may vary with policy if the assumption of exogeneity is not actually justified. It is a complete waste of time for the authorities to predict what will be the result of a change in policy when that prediction relies on the assumption of stability of parameters which *will, in fact*, change as a result of the policy change.

It may seem to the student that this problem is of minor significance. However, there are several episodes in recent British economic history where it has to be taken seriously, *viz* the failure to anticipate the inflationary effect of the 1967 devaluation; the misunderstanding of the impact of the 1971 Competition and Credit Control reforms on the monetary system; the Barber 'dash for growth' which had no visible impact on manufacturing investment; the change in the price–output dynamics of the economy which resulted from the adoption of floating exchange rates; the over-appreciation of sterling in 1979-80 which was associated with a 17% decline in manufacturing output in one year. It is more than bad luck that just about every macroeconomic relationship broke down in the 1970s. Such breakdowns should be expected whenever there is a major change in the policy environment as actors adjust their behaviour to the new environment.

According to the New Classical school, the search should be for 'policy invariant' models, i.e. models which are based upon the optimising behaviour of actors in such a way that the reaction of behaviour to policy changes can be explicitly accounted for. This is one of the reasons for the insistence on 'rationality' as a characteristic of the decision making of the typical actor. If behaviour was sub-optimal, then presumably reactions to policy changes would be arbitrary and unpredictable. It remains to be seen, of course, whether the New Classical school is any better placed to achieve structurally stable models than their antecedents. However, they have at least provided a great service in putting the issue at the top of the agenda. It would be disheartening, indeed, to believe that there were no routes to structural stability. However, economists should clearly be cautious about giving policy advice on the basis of the past performance of some model.

Expectations

The importance of expectations has long been appreciated by macroeconomists. In early Keynesian macroeconomics they arose most importantly in the analysis of investment. For example, since building a factory takes time there will be a delay before output is produced. So the entrepreneur has to form expectations about the demand for the product in the future in order to assess the likely profitability of the venture. More recently, an important role for expectations has arisen in the context of wage and price setting behaviour. This is because in negotiating wage contracts, for example, agents need to have some view about future changes in the value of money in order to assess the real value of any settlement. This issue will be discussed more fully in Chapter 6 below.

The problem posed by the presence of expectations takes the same form wherever it arises in the explicit formulation of testable models. When the expected value of some variable appears in an equation something has to be done about it because that variable is unobservable. A common method of solving this problem has been to extrapolate the past behaviour of the variable itself. In other words, take the past trend in the variable and assume that the trend will continue. A specific form of extrapolation is provided by the 'error learning mechanism' or 'adaptive expectations'. This says that the forecast currently being made of next periods value of the variable in question is a revision of the forecast made last period for the current period. The size of this revision is proportional to the error made last time and is in the same direction. If the expectation was, for example, of the price level, we would write:

4.1 $\quad p_t^e - p_{t-1}^e = \lambda(p_{t-1} - p_{t-1}^e) \qquad 0 < \lambda < 1$

The difference between the expectation of the price level in period t and expectation in period $t-1$ depends on the difference between the *actual outturn*, p_{t-1}, in $t-1$ and the expectation of what that would be. The time subscripts refer to the period of the outcome. The expectation is formed immediately prior to that.

This may not look very helpful as a way of replacing an unobservable variable by observables. Since

4.2 $\quad p_t^e = \lambda p_{t-1} + (1-\lambda) p_{t-1}^e$

we would be replacing one unobservable with an expression which contains another. However, since it is also true that:

4.3 $\quad p_{t-1}^e = \lambda p_{t-2} + (1-\lambda) p_{t-2}^e$

by continued substitutions we can obtain

4.4 $\quad p_t^e = \lambda p_{t-1} + \lambda(1-\lambda) p_{t-2} + \lambda(1-\lambda)^2 p_{t-3}$
$\qquad + \ldots + \lambda(1-\lambda)^n p_{t-n-1} + (1-\lambda)^{n+1} p_{t-n-1}^e$

The right-hand side of this expression only contains observables, except for the last term $(1-\lambda)^{n+1} p_{t-n-1}^e$. Since λ is less than unity, $(1-\lambda)^{n+1}$ will become very small as n gets larger. So if a large enough number of lagged values is used this last term can be ignored. The expectation of the variable is then replaced by a weighted average of past observations, the weights being geometrically declining.

One thing to notice immediately about adaptive expectations is that the only information used in forming them is the past observations on the variable in question. No other information is presumed to be of assistance. It would not be permissible, for example, for actors to expect higher prices just because OPEC announces a substantial rise in the price of oil today. They would have to wait until this had worked through to prices in the shops. The second thing to notice is that until prices have been stable for a considerable time, expectations formed adaptively will be consistently incorrect. This is because there is only a partial adjustment in response to the error in forecasting. Hence, there will only be no error in the steady state when the variable to be forecast is constant for some time.

The rational expectation (Muth 1961) of a variable is defined in such a way that it cannot be *systematically* incorrect. Formally, the rational expectation is the mathematical expectation given the information available at the time the expectation is formed:

4.5 $\quad p_t^e = E(p_t | I_{t-1})$

where E is the expectations operator, p_t^e is the typical actor's subjective expectation of the price level in period t, formed on the basis of all information available up to and including period $t-1$, I_{t-1}. In other words, the actors expectations will be the same as the best forecast that could be made with the information available when the forecast is made. This is what was meant by the statement that actors do 'the best they can'. It does not follow that the rational expectation will typically be correct, but it does follow that over-predictions and under-predictions will average out to zero, unless the information set is changing.

4.6 $\quad p_t^e = p_t + \epsilon_t \qquad E(\epsilon_t) = 0, \; E(\epsilon_t \epsilon_{t-i}) = 0 \text{ for all } i \neq 0$

The expectation will be equal to the actual value plus a random error with mean zero. If the error were not random the actor could improve his forecast by incorporating that information, i.e. he would learn from his mistakes.

It is sometimes argued in criticism of rational expectations that it is unreasonable to expect actors to be able to forecast as well as the best professional. Criticisms of this kind miss the point. Rationality implies no more than that the expectation is formed as the outcome of an optimisation exercise. In this respect it is no more extreme than the assumption of profit maximisation or utility maximisation. If information is freely available people will use it optimally. If information is not freely available they will acquire only just as much as it is worth their while to acquire. *It is only in specific applications of the idea that it is possible to say if the information required is in excess of that which it is reasonable to believe actors have.*

Aggregate Supply

While most of the early arguments between Monetarists and Keynesians were about the determinants of aggregate demand, an important characteristic of the New Classical school has been their formulation of the aggregate supply curve. A fairly standard version of this would be:

4.7 $\quad Y_t = \bar{Y} + \gamma \, (p_t - {}_{t-1}p_t^e)$

where Y_t is the level of output (national income) in period t, $\bar{Y}$ is the constant 'natural' level of output associated with the vertical Classical aggregate supply curve, p_t is the price level or the rate of inflation in period t and ${}_{t-1}p_t^e$ is the price level or the rate of inflation expected to hold in period t, when that expectation is formed on the basis of information available in period $t-1$. This says that there will be a fixed level of output except to the extent that actors make errors about prices. Notice that we can talk equivalently about inflation or the price level because

4.8 $\quad (p_t - p_{t-1}) - ({}_{t-1}p_t^e - p_{t-1}) = (p_t - {}_{t-1}p_t^e)$

and these variables are normally written in natural logarithms so that $p_t - p_{t-1}$ is the rate of inflation.

There are two somewhat different approaches in the literature which can be used to justify an aggregate supply curve of the form above. The first is due to Lucas and Rapping (1969) and underlies many of the New Classical explanations of the business cycle (see Chapter 8). It focuses explicitly on labour supply behaviour. Workers are presumed to have some notion of the normal wage, which may be thought of as the expected average wage. They have some flexibility as to how much they work, but in any given period more work means less leisure. Leisure yields positive utility, but so do the consumer goods they buy with their wages. In each period they have to decide how much to work, and they do so by comparing the current wage with the expected or normal wage. If the current wage is higher than the normal wage they will work more now in the expectation of taking more leisure in the future when the reward for working is expected to be lower. If the current wage is lower than normal they will take leisure now and expect to work more in the future when the reward is higher – in other words, there is inter-temporal substitution. This behaviour may reasonably be called 'speculative' labour supply. (Keynesian 'speculative' demand for money depends on comparing the current interest rate to the 'normal' interest rate.)

Thus, if the current wage is higher than expected more labour supply will be forthcoming and *vice versa*. The wage in question in both cases is presumed to be a real wage. The only way the price level (as compared to its expectation) enters into the Lucas/Rapping analysis is through its effect on the real interest rate. The real interest rate is important in its role as a way of discounting utility tomorrow into utility today. The expected real interest rate is defined as $r_t - \ln(p_t^e/p_t)$, where r_t is the current nominal interest rate, p_t^e is the expected price level and p_t is the actual price level. Lucas and Rapping argue that labour supply will be positively related to the expected real interest rate, and it is from this that labour supply would rise, with $(\ln p_t - \ln p_t^e)$ for a given nominal interest rate. This connection must surely be extremely tenuous. It is hard to believe that labour supply is much affected by the real interest rate and it is far from obvious what the sign of that effect would be. It is even far from obvious what the effect of a change in expected inflation would be on the expected real interest rate.

While the precise link between the Lucas/Rapping analysis and 'unanticipated price changes' is rather tenuous, the spirit is less so. This is that a demand shock which is perceived to be temporary will have an effect on current supply which is greater than that which would result from a permanent demand shift. This is because of the inter-temporal substitution of work into the period when demand is high and away from the (future) period when demand is (expected to be) lower. We shall return to this issue in the context of discussions of the business cycle below. Notice in passing, however, that the Lucas/Rapping analysis depends in no way on rational expectation; indeed, they use adaptive expectations to determine the 'normal' level of wages and prices. What they do assume, however, is that prices and wages clear markets in each period. So changes in employment are perceived as 'voluntary' in the sense that everyone who would choose to work at current wage rates can do so. This is a source of some controversy which we shall return to below.

The second approach to aggregate supply is that to be found in

Lucas (1972, 1973). Here the focus is directly on goods markets rather than on labour markets. Sellers are presumed to be located in one of a large number of 'local' markets which are segregated, though within each market there is perfect competition. The local price is known for the current period, but the general price level across all markets is only learned with a lag. The problem for the seller is to decide how much to sell (and produce) when he observes the current price. This is difficult because a change in price could reflect a shift in demand towards his market (to which he should rationally respond) or merely a change in the value of money (to which he should not respond). Part of the decision, therefore, depends upon a single comparison of the current local price with the *expectation* of the general price level for the same period. If they are the same there is certainly no reason to change his supply. If they are different he may wish to change his supply. However, the size of his response will depend upon his perceptions as to the variability of the price level as compared to the variability of relative price changes. It is here that rational expectations enter the scene, since the actor is presumed to optimally respond to this price signal in the light of knowledge of the 'true' probability distribution of price level changes and real demand shifts. If the variance of price level changes is high relative to the variance of demand shifts (they are assumed to be statistically independent), the price signals should be distrusted and the supply response should be small. If the reverse is true a change in current price is more likely to reflect a real shock to which supply should respond. Therefore, γ above (equation 4.7) will be close to zero if price level changes have a high variance relative to the variance of real shocks. It will be significantly above zero if the reverse is true.

While providing a formal justification of the 'surprise' aggregate supply curve, this argument is not entirely convincing either, even though the supply curve itself has almost become 'conventional wisdom'. The problem is that the restriction of information it requires is just as *ad hoc* as many of the alternative Keynesian stories such as sticky money wages. Why should a seller perceive the demand price for the product earlier than he perceives the general price level? It is quite possible that the reverse would be true. Aggregate information and forecasts are much more widely available than information on specific markets.

An alternative explanation of this supply curve is based upon an asymmetry of information between workers and firms. This is the approach mentioned in Chapter 1 above. Demand for labour by firms depends upon the real wage where both the money wage and the price of output are correctly perceived. Labour supply depends upon the real wage. Workers perceive the money wage correctly, but their belief about the purchasing power of that wage depends upon their *expectation* of the price level. An unexpected increase in aggregate demand will lead to an increase in aggregate supply. Initially, prices will rise by more than money wages. Firms will correctly perceive this as a fall in the real wage and will demand more labour. Workers will *incorrectly* perceive a rise in the real wage and will supply more labour. The higher labour input will be associated with higher output, that is, greater aggregate supply. Whether or not expectations are rational, this effect can only be temporary as workers are unlikely to be fooled for long.

Again, this seems a somewhat tenuous basis for the theory of aggregate supply. Supply will only change if someone is tricked. However, some thought about the supply side structure within which this result is derived will show why it must emerge in that framework. It is the characterisation of the economy which must be challenged to overthrow the result, not the internal consistency of the analysis itself. In an economy with one input and one output there is only one relative price – the real wage. The market clearing real wage is unique (if both labour supply and demand depend on it) and that is all there is to it. Without more structure to the economy there is no scope for real changes in output and employment, especially in response to nominal expenditures. This, of course, is why Keynes thought Classical economics to be unsatisfactory. The real problem is to explain why output and employment do actually fluctuate. We shall return to this central question when discussing business cycles in Chapter 8.

Policy Ineffectiveness

The supply function is important because the New Classical claim concerning the ineffectiveness of systematic aggregate demand policy depends upon it.

Consider figure 4.1. The economy is initially at p_0 $\overline{Y}$, with aggregate demand D_0. The level of income $\overline{Y}$ is the 'natural' level of

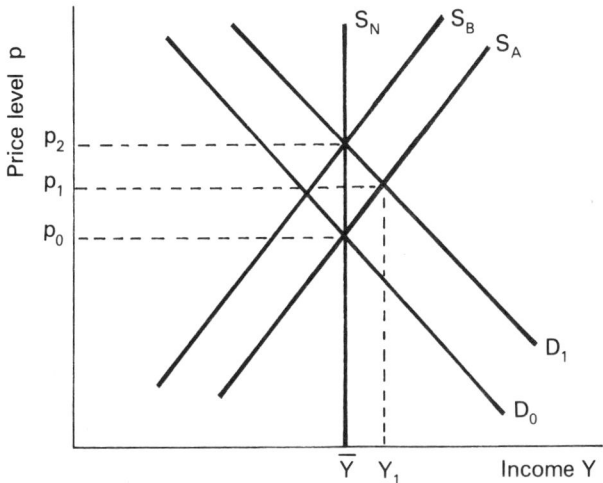

Figure 4.1

output which is defined to be that sustainable in the long run. Any greater level will be associated with rising prices. The supply curve S_A will be the response to an unanticipated shift in D. This is because, with p^e held constant, the curve of equation 4.7 has a positive slope with respect to p_t. However, as p_t^e is revised upwards S_A will shift to the left. With rational expectations, p_t^e will not differ from p_t for any reason that could be predicted. Hence, if a shift in aggregate demand is anticipated all its effect will be felt in prices and not in output. The economy will go straight from p_0 to p_2, but $\overline{Y}$ will not change.

In this framework any systematic policy reactions which involve shifting aggregate demand will have no real effect – at least where the authorities respond with a lag and they are not better informed than the actors. Consider again equation 4.7, which is modified only by adding a random supply disturbance e_t^s:

4.9 $\quad Y_t = \overline{Y} + \gamma \, (p_t - p_t^e) + e_t^s$

The price level can be assumed to be proportional to the money stock M_t, plus a random demand disturbance, e_t^d:

4.10 $\quad p_t = \alpha M_t + e_t^d$

Let us suppose that the monetary authorities keep the money stock constant, except that they try to stabilise the economy by changing the money stock in response to deviations of the last period's output from the natural rate. They achieve this with a random error, e_t^M.

4.11 $M_t = \beta_0 + \beta_1 (\bar{Y} - Y_{t-1}) + e_t^M$

With rational expectations, actors will expect the price level to be proportional to the systematic component of the money stock.

4.12 $p_t^e = \alpha(\beta_0 + \beta_1 (\bar{Y} - Y_{t-1}))$

The actual price level will also depend on the error in 4.11 and the demand disturbance.

4.13 $p_t = \alpha(\beta_0 + \beta_1 (\bar{Y} - Y_{t-1})) + \alpha\, e_t^M + e_t^d$

So the error in price expectations just depends on the disturbances – subtract 4.12 from 4.13.

4.14 $p_t - p_t^e = \alpha\, e_t^M + e_t^d$

Substituting this back into 4.9 results in the following:

4.15 $Y_t - \bar{Y} = \gamma \alpha\, e_t^M + \gamma\, e_t^d + e_t^s$

This says that the deviation of current real income from the natural rate only depends upon the random disturbances and not at all upon the systematic component of policy. This is essentially the analysis of Sargent and Wallace (1975) which leads to the conclusion that only unanticipated policy matters.

An obvious comment on this result is that if deviations from the natural rate (of output or unemployment) were really random then stabilisation policy would not be necessary anyway. It is persistent deviations that have to be explained and, of course, corrected for. New Classical economists would all accept that there has to be persistence and, indeed, assume it (and discover it) in their empirical work. If they did not do so their case would hardly be credible. Lucas (1973), for example, writes his aggregate supply curve:

4.16 $\quad Y_t - \overline{Y}_t = \gamma(p_t - p_t^e) + \lambda(Y_{t-1} - \overline{Y}_{t-1})$

where the term $\lambda(Y_{t-1} - \overline{Y}_{t-1})$ reflects persistence, though this persistence is not justified explicitly and must, therefore, be considered *ad hoc*. However, even though random shocks lead to sustained output changes this does not restore a role for systematic stabilisation policy, as repeating the above exercise with 4.15 instead of 4.9 will demonstrate.

One line of argument that will restore at least partial policy effectiveness is that of long-term overlapping wage contracts (Fischer 1977, Taylor 1979, 1980). This works by creating some stickiness in money wages and thereby allowing some temporary real wage changes which can be exploited by the authorities. Suppose, for example, that money wage contracts are set for two periods and the authorities continue to operate the rule 4.12. Wage contracts will presumably reflect price expectations over the subsequent two periods, but they cannot anticipate the systematic reaction of the authorities in the second period because this depends on the outcome in the first period which has not yet happened. Thus, aggregate demand policies will exert some leverage over aggregate supply in the short term. This effect will die out over time as the longest contract matures and money wages catch up with prices.

The proposition that only 'unanticipated policy has real effects' has some *prima facie* support due to work by Barro (1977, 1978). On annual data for the US for the period 1941–1973, Barro shows that the unemployment rate is significantly affected by unanticipated money growth, but that it is either unaffected or affected perversely by actual money growth. Unanticipated money growth is measured as the difference between the actual and fitted values of an equation in which money growth depends upon its own lagged values, the deviation of the Federal budget deficit from normal and lagged unemployment. This is a mixture of a kind of reaction function and budget constraint. Unanticipated money growth has effects not only in the same year, but also in two subsequent years and, thus, illustrates the importance of persistence. Actual money growth has no significant negative effect on lowering unemployment, except a marginal one after four years. The overall fit is much worse than for unanticipated money. Similar results are available for the UK (Attfield, Demery and Duck 1981).

Impressive as these results are, they are not entirely convincing. Indeed, the method of generating 'unanticipated' money growth is inconsistent with rational expectations. Information should only be used which was available at the time. There may be no relation between the residual in 1948 of an equation estimated with a sample for, say, 1946 to 1973 and the forecast error that would have been made in 1948 based only upon information available in 1947. My forecast of next year cannot be dependent on information that will only become available subsequently. Barro notes this point, but does not cope with it.

Secondly, the news that the rate of growth of money does not explain unemployment will be quite happily received by Keynesians, Monetarists and New Classical economists alike, though for very different reasons. The story that only unanticipated money matters is more troublesome until it is realised that this is consistent with a completely different scenario. Suppose the authorities are pegging interest rates rather than controlling the money stock (fixing the exchange rate will do just as well). *Real disturbances* will then *cause* monetary changes rather than *vice versa*. In so far as the real disturbances are uncorrelated with earlier monetary growth, the current monetary change will be unpredictable by any monetary rule. Here, of course, causation runs exactly in reverse and so constitutes a very different kind of explanation. This substitute explanation must have some *prima facie* plausibility in the light of the widespread practice of stabilising both interest rates and exchange rates in the bulk of the sample periods studied so far, though this evidence is at least consistent with the New Classical view.

Summary

New Classical economics is a major source of ideas which are a challenge to both Keynesians and Monetarists alike. As advocates of rational expectations New Classical economists are on strong ground, especially if the notion is applied carefully (i.e. with limited, or even endogenous, information). One important area of application is that of exchange rates which will be discussed below. Rather harder to accept is their portrait of the supply structure of the macroeconomy. Here, the insistence of continuous market clearing in a 'natural rate' framework so that only 'surprises' matter seems unnecessarily nihilistic. We shall have more to say on these subjects below.

PART III
Issues

The central issues of macroeconomics are, as they have always been, inflation and unemployment. These are the subject of Chapter 6. The understanding of these issues is difficult without some appreciation of the role of the external environment. Chapter 5, accordingly, discusses the balance of payments and exchange rates. Chapters 7 and 8 discuss the impact of government on the economy through crowding out and as a cause or curer of business cycles. Chapter 9 points to the importance of supply shocks. Chapter 10 is by way of summary of the major themes.

5
Balance of Payments and Exchange Rates

The dominant constraint on macroeconomic policy in the UK in the 1950s and 1960s was perceived to be the balance of payments. The nature of this constraint changed in the early 1970s as a result of the adoption of floating exchange rates by the major industrial countries. The sterling exchange rate has been floating continuously since June 1972, though the UK authorities may have influenced it from time to time. What was the nature of the 'balance of payments constraint'? Why has the economy fared worse under floating exchange rates? It is worth recalling that many economists in the 1950s and 1960s advocated a switch to floating exchange rates. This, they claimed, would eliminate the balance of payments constraint and facilitate the pursuit of expansionist policies. In the decade after floating (1972–1982) there was virtually no real growth. Indeed, there was an absolute decline in industrial production.

How, then, should the balance of payments be perceived and what difference does it make if the exchange rate is floating?

The Keynesian or Structural Approach

The Keynesian approach is based upon an analysis of the balance of trade. In its simplest form it relies on a single import function and a single export function such as equations 1.3 and 1.4. If we specify the import function so that imports are proportional to income as in equation 1.3,

5.1 $P = \gamma Y$

while exports, X_0, remain exogenously determined, then the balance of payments can be analysed simply in the context of figure 5.1. Since exports are constant and imports rise with national income, the balance of payments gets steadily worse as national income rises. Beyond a national income of Y_1 the balance of payments is in deficit.

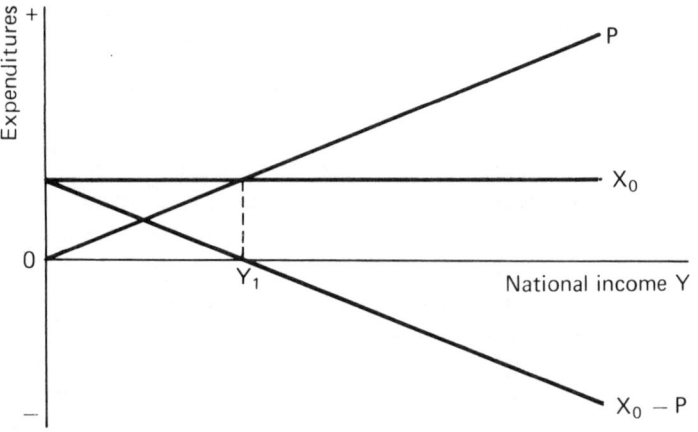

Figure 5.1

While this model is a gross over-simplification, it represents a view of the economy which was widely held and which would appear to have been justified by UK experience. Any tendency for over-expansion in the UK economy produced balance of payments problems. The experience of the Stop–Go cycle in the UK throughout the 1950s and 1960s seemed to confirm the story that domestic expansion increased imports faster than exports, so the balance of payments inevitably deteriorated. As a result, the expansion had to be reversed. One curiosity, however, to which we shall return, is why it is that this pattern did not seem to apply to other countries? How was it that countries like West Germany and Japan expanded so fast without running into balance of payments problems? Indeed, West Germany at one time had exactly the opposite problem – its economic success was associated with an almost perpetual balance of payments surplus.

Most Keynesian models of the balance of payments, such as those used for forecasting, would, of course, be more complex than that above. Exports and imports would typically be broken down into several different categories and there would be an equation for each. The form of equation would, however, be similar for each category. Exports depend upon foreign demand and relative prices and imports depend upon domestic demand and relative prices. The overall balance of payments forecast would be obtained by combining all of these import and export categories which had been forecast separately. These categories normally represent different industrial sectors. Hence, this can be thought of as a 'structural' approach.

Many operational models of the balance of payments had similar properties to the aggregate expenditure model above. An expansion of domestic aggregate demand worsens the balance of payments and the addition of a relative price effect can only serve to reinforce this. However, the structural approach to the balance of payments does allow a bias to develop in attributing blame for balance of payments problems. Since the core of the balance of payments is the real trade account, failure here must be due to 'inadequate' export performance, these inadequacies being attributable either to unenterprising businessmen or myopic trade unions which escalate wages and make export prices 'uncompetitive'. An alternative approach points the finger directly at government macroeconomic policy as the source of the problem. This is the monetary approach which is discussed below.

Mundell's Assignment Problem

One major inadequacy of the Keynesian approach to the balance of payments is that it focuses entirely upon the current account. Systematic interactions between the capital account and the domestic economy are thereby completely ignored. A simple rectification of this omission, in the IS-LM framework, was proposed by Mundell (1968). This treatment still provides the basis of many textbook models of the balance of payments. Ignoring capital flows was, perhaps, excusable in the 1950s since there was not general convertibility of major currencies and, as a result, private capital flows were of minimal significance. However, by 1971 financial capital movements were potentially so large that many observers attributed the breakdown of the fixed exchange rate system to their very size and volatility.

The Mundell model is achieved by adding to Model II of Chapter 1 a relationship between net capital flows and the domestic interest rate:

5.2 $k = f(r)$

Net capital flows depend upon the interest rate.

Capital flows should not be thought of as sales of machines to foreigners, rather they are net sales to foreigners of domestic bonds. There is a problem in drawing the line between the current and capital accounts. In this case 'capital' includes only financial assets. Assuming foreign interest rates to be fixed exogenously, as the domestic interest rate rises foreigners will buy more domestic bonds so the capital account of the balance of payments will improve. In effect, foreigners are lending more to the domestic economy.

The overall balance of payments is the current account plus the capital account. The current account gets worse as national income rises just as in the Keynesian model. Thus, if balance of payments equilibrium is to be maintained (at zero overall) as national income rises, the domestic rate of interest must also rise so that the improved capital account compensates for the worsening current account. In other words, the locus of zero overall balance of payments positions will be a positive relationship between national income and the interest rate, like BB in figure 5.2.

Equilibrium for the system as a whole requires that all three lines BB, LM and IS should intersect at the same point. Consider the policy choices in the initial situation depicted in figure 5.2. The IS and LM curves intersect at A where there is full employment. However, this is not a point of balance of payments equilibrium, since A is to the right of the BB curve. In fact there is a balance of payments deficit at A equal to the horizontal distance between A and BB multiplied by the marginal propensity to import. It is open to the authorities to correct the deficit by appropriate use of monetary and fiscal policy, but it is not obvious which to use.

A fiscal deflation would move the economy to point C, whereas a

BALANCE OF PAYMENTS AND EXCHANGE RATES 91

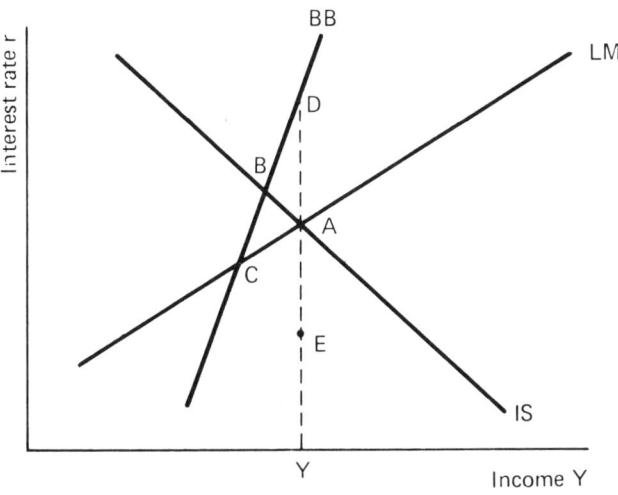

Figure 5.2

contraction of the money supply would move it to point B. Mundell's point is that the best response is to react with monetary policy to the balance of payments and with fiscal policy to output (and thus to unemployment). Consider the contrary. Initially we react to the balance of payments deficit by shifting IS down until it passes through C. This has corrected the balance of payments but caused unemployment. An increase in money supply now designed to eliminate unemployment would shift the LM curve down to the right. The economy would then be at a point like E where the balance of payments deficit is *worse* than it was originally. If, however, starting from A we change the money supply in response to a balance of payments deficit and fiscal policy in response to unemployment, the economy would converge on point D at which there is full employment and balance of payments equilibrium. This is the reason for Mundell's assignment of monetary policy to the balance of payments and fiscal policy to output and employment.

Mundell's model should be thought of as a textbook model which imparts many useful insights but remains an over-simplification. One major criticism that has been levelled at it is that the capital flow equation is inconsistent with portfolio theory, which focuses on the demand for stocks. In the presence of uncertainty, an interest rate change will lead to a once-and-for-all adjustment of portfolios rather than a perpetual flow. However, at least the Mundell approach did include a monetary sector and as such was the first step in the evolution of a major critique of Keynesian balance of payments theory.

The Monetary Approach to the Balance of Payments

It has been seen that Keynesian balance of payments theory concentrates on the market for goods. The principal effect of an exogenous increase in exports would be to change income through the multiplier process. It was not always thus. In the classical world of David Hume trade deficits were associated directly with money supply changes.

Consider a pure gold standard world in which gold is both the internal and the external money. If the domestic economy developed a balance of payments surplus, a classical economist would point to the fact that the domestic gold stock would be rising by the amount of the surplus *per period*. In other words, any imbalance in the value of goods flows is matched by net money flows in the opposite direction. The adjustment process from here on would be automatic since the rise in the domestic money stock would raise domestic money prices and cause a substitution of foreign for domestic goods. Thus the balance of payments surplus would disappear. This is the price-specie flow mechanism of classical economics.

Notice that where the internal and external money is the same the balance of payments is not a problem *per se*. Outflows of bullion may have caused banking crises and contraction of the money stock may have caused unemployment, but the balance of payments was no more a problem in the pure gold standard world than the balance of payments of East Anglia is today. There was, of course, a problem when paper backed by gold began to circulate as money, because external payments required bullion. As a result, the reserve ratios of banks came under pressure whenever gold left the country. However, this was not an 'official sector' problem as reserve outflows under fixed exchange rates would be today. In the modern world, where each nation state has its own fiat money, it might be thought that there has ceased to be a connection between the domestic money stock and the balance of payments. However, this is not true if the authorities are intervening to support the domestic exchange rate.

The process of pegging an exchange rate means that, in the UK case, the Bank of England takes up the residual excess demand or supply of foreign exchange at or close to the pegged price. If the UK had a balance of payments surplus, the authorities would buy foreign exchange with newly issued sterling. The foreign money would go into reserves and the sterling would go into the domestic money supply so long as it is spent on UK goods. The new increase in the money supply could be 'sterilised' by open market bond sales but this is of limited use since the process of selling more government debt would raise domestic interest rates and thereby induce additional capital inflows which would increase the balance of payments surplus still further.

The monetary approach points out that since the balance of payments has monetary effects, and is indeed a monetary 'problem', the domestic demand for money (or indeed other assets) should be an integral part of balance of payments analysis. If money continues to flow across the international exchanges then domestic money markets cannot be in equilibrium. An excess supply of money domestically will be reflected in an outflow across the exchanges. As the absorption approach emphasised, the balance of payments on current accounts is by definition equal to the difference between what the economy earns (output) and what it spends (national expenditure). Any group or individual for whom income and spending differ will be changing asset holdings. The decisions to spend or save out of a given income are not independent. However, specifying asset choices and expenditure decisions simultaneously offers important insights. The Keynesian approach focused explicitly on expenditures. The monetary approach emphasised asset stocks, especially money.

The most influential single contribution to the monetary approach is that of Johnson (1976). He considers a highly simplified world in which there are rigidly fixed exchange rates and all goods are traded at a single world price. Real income growth is exogenous. The domestic money demand function is given by:

5.3 $\quad M_d = p.f(Y,r)$

> Real money demand depends upon real income and the rate of interest.

And the money supply is given by definition as the sum of money domestically created and money associated with international reserve changes.

5.4 $\quad M_s = R + D$

> Money stock is equal to reserves plus domestic credit.

If the system is in static equilibrium money demand will equal money supply and there will be no reserve changes. If, however, domestic income is perpetually growing, with constant world prices and interest rates, Johnson shows that the growth in reserves will be *positively* related to domestic income growth and *negatively* related to domestic credit expansion.

5.5 $\quad g_R = \alpha_0 \eta_y g_y - \alpha_1 g_D$

where g_R, g_y and g_D are the growth rates of reserves, income and domestic credit respectively, and η_y is the income elasticity of demand for money.

This is a remarkable conclusion which implies that real income growth *alone* improves the balance of payments and is in stark contrast to the Keynesian model above, where a rise in income has exactly the opposite effect. How does this result come about? Very simply, if there is real income growth, at constant price and interest rate levels, then there will be growing demand for money for transactions purposes. An excess demand for money can be met in one of two ways, either through domestic credit creation or through a balance of payments surplus. If there is no domestic credit expansion, reserve will grow in line with the growth in money demand. The existence of an excess demand for money means that people will be spending less than their income. For the country as a whole there will be a balance of payments surplus. If, on the other hand, domestic credit expands faster than money demand, then there will be a loss of reserves through a balance of payments deficit. The problem, then, which causes balance of payments deficits and associated reserve losses is not income expansion itself but rather the authorities' policies with respect to domestic credit expansion. If domestic credit expands faster than demand for money balances, there will be a balance of payments deficit and associated reserve losses.

The monetary approach under fixed exchange rates should be thought of as a theory of reserve changes rather than the trade balance, since it is not clear from the literature whether the effects will appear in the current or capital account. However, it should be obvious that many of the simplifying assumptions in the Johnson model are not at all critical. Indeed, a wide range of possible macroeconomic models will have similar properties, at least in the long run, so long as they include a monetary sector which generates a stock demand for money.

The monetary approach does, however, resolve for us the apparent paradox of fast growing countries which appear to have perpetual balance of payments surpluses, though it does not tell us where this growth comes from. Indeed this approach predicts exactly this outcome, so long as the domestic monetary authority restricts the growth of domestic credit to less than the growth in money demand. Thus in countries like West Germany in the 1960s, since the fast growth in real income caused a growth in transactions demand for money, the economy induced an inflow of money via the foreign balance to the extent that this money was not created by the Central Bank. Since the economy was trying to acquire financial assets it would be spending less than the value of its output which is identical to running a balance of payments surplus. This surplus could be sustained because growing income required ever-growing money balances. The UK problem was the opposite – slow real growth and faster domestic credit expansion leading to perpetual balance of payments problems.

Flexible Exchange Rates

Much of the above discussion has presumed the existence of fixed exchange rates. The widespread variability of exchange rates since 1971 has required a great deal more attention to be paid to flexible exchange rates and their policy implications. In the Keynesian type models the exchange rate is treated as an exogenous variable which has two effects. The first effect is that, in so far as it changes the

96 CONTROVERSIES IN MACROECONOMICS

terms of trade or competitiveness, it causes changes in imports and exports. Secondly, a fall in the exchange rate *causes* inflation through the import cost component of prices.

An endogenous treatment of the exchange rate, of course, requires an explicit model of the market in which it is determined – the international money market. The modern literature on the exchange rate developed out of the monetary approach to the balance of payments. A collection of work in this area is provided in Frenkel and Johnson (1978).

The traditional textbook analysis of the exchange rate derives certain propositions about the *flow* demand for foreign exchange from the demands for imports and exports. Suppose there are two countries, the UK and the US. There is trade in goods between them. Each has a different domestic currency and the domestic currency price of domestic output is assumed to be fixed. The UK demands US goods but the sterling price in the UK depends upon how much UK citizens have to pay for dollars. The higher the price of dollars, the more expensive will be US goods in the UK, and vice versa. UK citizens demand a flow of dollars to pay for their imports and US citizens demand a flow of sterling to pay for UK exports.

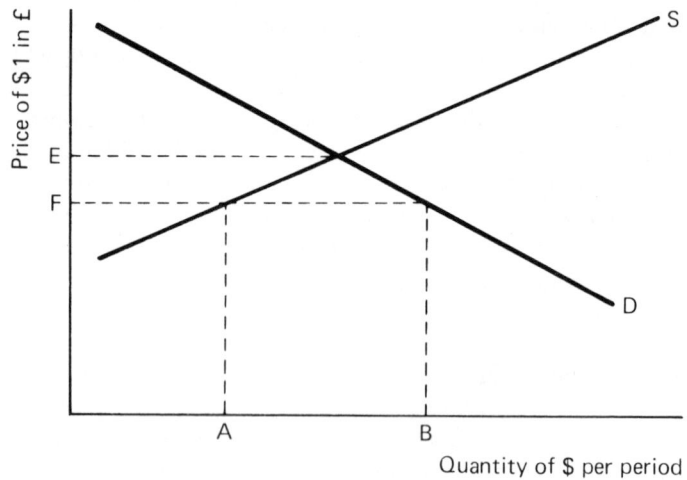

Figure 5.3

In figure 5.3 the vertical axis shows the price of $1 in pounds, so going up the axis is devaluing the pound. The horizontal axis shows the quantity of dollars demanded or supplied in exchange for pounds. As the price of dollars rises UK citizens find the price of US goods has gone up, so they buy less of them. If demand is elastic they will buy both a smaller quantity and a *smaller value* and will, therefore, demand fewer dollars. In that case the demand curve for dollars D will be downward sloping with respect to the exchange rate. Even if the underlying demand curve for goods were negatively sloped, the demand curve for dollars would be upward sloping if the demand for goods were not elastic.

The supply of dollars, S, is upward sloping so long as US demand for UK goods is elastic, since they will buy a greater value of British goods as the pound is devalued. This is basically the elasticity approach to the balance of payments and it leads to the Marshall–Lerner condition. This is that for a devaluation to improve the balance of payments, the sum of the elasticities of demand for imports and exports must exceed one in absolute value. This is really the stability condition for the market depicted in figure 5.3, since if D were upward sloping and S downward sloping the market would be unstable in the sense that there would be excess demand above the equilibrium price and excess supply below.

This model is extremely helpful in illustrating why the balance of payments is such a problem when the authorities are trying to peg the exchange rate in an overvalued position, such as at F. Here there is an excess demand for dollars, which in this model is the same as a current account deficit, equal to $B-A$. The only way that the price F can be maintained is by the domestic authorities providing $B-A$ dollars per period out of reserves by, in effect, buying back sterling of equivalent value. Reserves are finite so this position is not sustainable indefinitely. A short-term solution is to borrow more reserves. A devaluation would involve changing the intervention price to E. But the conventional response in the 1950s and early 1960s was to depress domestic expenditures so that the D curve would be shifted to the left.

The monetary approach is critical of treating exchange rates as solely determined by flow demand for currencies derived from flow demands for goods. Exchange rates are the relative price of two moneys, so conditions in money markets must have some part to play. In a world of mobile financial capital the critical condition to be met is that all money stocks and financial asset stocks must be willingly held, at the margin. If there are excess money supplies or portfolio disequilibria, then financial capital will be flowing internationally and, in the absence of central bank intervention, exchange rates will be changing.

The principal difference between the fixed and floating exchange rate cases of the monetary approach is that, in the former, the price level was fixed to that of the rest of the world and the nominal money supply could change through induced reserve changes. In the latter there are no reserve changes and the nominal domestic money supply is fixed by the authorities. However, the *real* money supply is determined endogenously because domestic prices are no longer tied to foreign prices. Monetary expansion by the authorities now leads to downward pressure on the exchange rate and upward pressure on the domestic price level. The exchange rate measures the value of domestic money in terms of other moneys. The price level measures the value of domestic money in terms of goods. They are both indicators of the same thing – declining value of the domestic money. Neither is the cause of inflation, both are different aspects of the same inflation.

The monetary approach to the exchange rate does not claim that only monetary factors are important, but it does stress the importance of money markets in the short-run determination of exchange rates. This is because it may take a long time for price changes to influence goods markets, but the international 'wholesale' money markets are highly sensitive to minute interest differentials and expected exchange rate changes. If these markets anticipate an exchange rate change as a result of, say, some policy change, holders will tend to move immediately out of the currency which is expected to decline in value. Floating currencies do not move smoothly in line with inflation differentials. They adjust quickly to new information, but with a tendency to overshoot. The cause of overshooting will be discussed below.

Finally, it is important to avoid confusion about whether the monetary approach is a long-run or short-run theory. The fixed rate case was criticised by some for only explaining the long-run situation, while the proponents of the floating case espouse it as providing the dominant short-run explanation of exchange rates. It would seem that the behaviour of the authorities can change a model from long run to short run or vice versa. The answer to this paradox is very simple. In both cases transactions demand for money for most individuals and non-financial firms can be out of equilibrium for long periods. International goods arbitrage is also slow, so that the 'law of one price' or purchasing power parity are at best long-run equilibrium conditions. However, interest arbitrage equilibrium conditions as between financial firms such as international banks hold almost exactly even in the very short run. The monetary approach *in both fixed and floating exchange rate cases* is a theory of short-run international portfolio adjustments, i.e. capital flows. These markets adjust most quickly and can thus dominate exchange markets in the short run. They are thus vital components to the explanation of short-run exchange rate changes in one case and reserve changes in the other. In the long run wider influences come into play.

Exchange Rate Models: An Introduction

Considerable effort has been devoted in the last few years to analysing the behaviour of floating exchange rates. A collection of papers relevant to the UK experience is available in Eltis and Sinclair (1981). Some of the most important theoretical work in this area is due to Dornbusch (1976a, 1976b). Before discussing this theoretical work, however, it is important to emphasise that this area is not of peripheral importance for an understanding of recent UK economic history. Indeed, it would be hard to explain the dramatic rise in unemployment in the UK since 1979 without reference to the exchange rate. Unemployment will be discussed in the next chapter. Let us now devote attention to the exchange rate itself.

There is an important analytical distinction between models of the long-run behaviour of exchange rates and the short-run. For the long run, Purchasing Power Parity (PPP) is presumed to hold, so that prices of traded goods are the same in all countries (when converted at the existing exchange rate). There is no reason why PPP should hold in the short run, since it may take considerable time for goods arbitrage to react to price differentials. It is interest parity that ties down the exchange rate in the short run. The long run case will be examined first.

Consider a two country world where all goods are traded. Purchasing Power Parity holds so that prices in the domestic country will equal those in the foreign country when converted by the exchange rate.

$$5.6 \quad p = Ep^*$$

where p is the domestic price level, p^* is the foreign price level and E is the domestic currency price of one unit of foreign currency (pounds per dollar). Each economy has a demand for real money balances which depends upon real income.

$$5.7 \quad \frac{M}{p} = KY^\alpha \quad \text{and} \quad \frac{M^*}{p^*} = K^* Y^{*\beta}$$

where * denotes values for the foreign economy, K is the inverse of the velocity of circulation and α and β are the respective income elasticities of demand for real money balances.

Rearrange 5.7 as expressions for p and p^* and substitute into 5.6 so $M/KY^\alpha = E\, M^*/K^* Y^{*\beta}$. This gives

$$5.8 \quad E = \frac{M}{M^*} \cdot \frac{K^*}{K} \cdot \frac{Y^{*\beta}}{Y^\alpha}$$

The exchange rate, therefore, depends upon relative money stocks, relative velocity and relative real income. Converting all variables into growth rates (log differentials) we would have

$$5.9 \quad e = (m - m^*) + (k^* - k) + (\beta y^* - \alpha y)$$

This focuses attention for explaining the percentage rate of change of the exchange rate by regard for differences in monetary growth rates, velocity *changes* and income growth. This is the floating rate analogue of equation 5.5. If the rate of monetary expansion at home, *ceteris paribus*, is faster than that overseas e will rise. This is a devaluation of the home currency. Notice that the derivation depends critically upon 5.6 holding.

Equation 5.9 provides the framework for much of the recent empirical work on exchange rates (see Frenkel 1979 and Eltis and Sinclair 1981). However, a framework based upon PPP is unlikely to be very helpful in explaining short-run exchange rate movements. It is well known that exchange rates can move substantially and rapidly so that PPP is violated for significant periods. The problem is to explain this short-term volatility of exchange rates.

If the exchange rate is not tied down by the fact that goods have the same price in all markets, some other condition has to be used. The obvious one is interest parity. Interest parity requires that the expected return on assets of different currency denomination should be equal. If they were not equal funds would be moving and exchange rates would be changing. A full discussion of the nature of interest parity is beyond our present scope. It will simply be presumed to hold in a particular form and the implications will be pursued. Suffice it to say that there are forms of the interest parity relationship which do hold more or less exactly so long as appropriate interest rates are chosen. Critical for what follows is the assumption implicit in the dropping of PPP and adoption of interest parity. This is that asset markets adjust quickly and goods markets adjust slowly. Goods prices are sticky, but exchange rates and interest rates can change rapidly. The model to be discussed is essentially that due to Dornbusch (1976b).

Consider an IS–LM type portfolio choice between money and bonds. Domestic bonds and money are denominated in domestic currency (obviously) and foreign bonds and money are denominated in foreign currency. Interest parity requires that the expected return on domestic and foreign bonds be equal. If exchange rates can change, the relative return has two elements – the coupon interest yield and the change in the exchange rate.

5.10 $\quad r = r^* + x$

The domestic interest rate, r, is equal to the foreign rate, r^*, plus the expected rate of *depreciation* of the domestic currency. If, for example, the sterling bond interest is 5% per period and the equivalent dollar rate is 10%, sterling must be expected to depreciate by 5% per period. If this were not true it would be expected to be profitable to shift funds to where the return were higher. Notice, though, that the mere fact that one interest rate is higher does not indicate inequality of expected return.

The exchange rate is defined to adjust at some rate θ from the existing exchange rate e to the equilibrium $\bar{e}$.

5.11 $\quad x = \theta(\bar{e} - e)$

where e and $\bar{e}$ are now in logs. Again, we focus on the domestic money market as expressed by the demand for money equation (plus the assumption that supply equals demand).

5.12 $m - p = \alpha y - \lambda r$

where variables are in logs, except the interest rate, r. (This is the same as 5.7 if $K = \exp[-\lambda r]$.) The foreign economy can be assumed to be 'large' relative to the home economy. This enables us to take the foreign interest rate r^* as exogenously fixed. Substitute 5.11 into 5.10 for x and then substitute this combined expression into 5.12 for r. This gives

5.13 $m - p = \alpha y - \lambda r^* - \lambda\theta(\bar{e} - e)$

This is nothing more than the domestic money market clearing condition when interest parity is imposed as an extra constraint. Notice that in full equilibrium e will equal $\bar{e}$, so equilibrium prices will be:

5.14 $\bar{p} = m - \alpha y + \lambda r^*$

This enables us to simplify 5.13 by replacing $m - \alpha y + \lambda r^*$ with $\bar{p}$. Rearranging as an expression for the exchange rate gives

5.15 $e = \bar{e} - (\dfrac{1}{\lambda\theta})(p - \bar{p})$

This says that the exchange rate will deviate from the long-run level if the price level deviates from its long-run level. This may not seem particularly interesting, but in reality it says a great deal about the behaviour of exchange rates.

Consider figure 5.4. This plots two relationships between the price level and the exchange rate. The positive sloped (45°) line labelled $p = e$ is equation 5.6. This is determined by Purchasing Power Parity. It is drawn on the assumption that units are chosen so that p^* is unity.

The negative relation between p and e is given by equation 5.15 for given values of exogenous variable (so given values of $\bar{e}$ and $\bar{p}$). It reflects domestic money market clearing in conjunction with interest parity.

BALANCE OF PAYMENTS AND EXCHANGE RATES 103

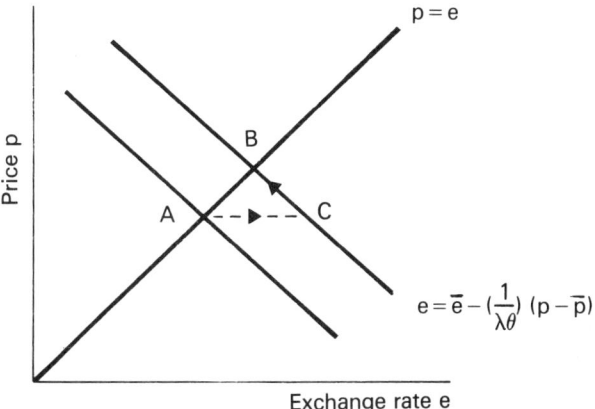

Figure 5.4

Start at *A* in full equilibrium and let there be a once-and-for-all rise in the domestic money stock. Let us presume that the domestic economy is at full employment so that income effects can be neglected (a vertical IS curve or a classical aggregate supply curve will do just as well.) From 5.14 and 5.6 it should be obvious that in full equilibrium both *p* and *e* will rise in proportion to the increase in *m*. (Recall that *e* is the domestic currency price of one unit of foreign exchange, so a rise in *e* is a devaluation of the domestic currency.) This means that the new money market clearing condition will pass through a point like *B* which is north-east of *A*.

However, the economy will only jump straight to *B* if prices and exchange rates are perfectly flexible. In that case the excess money stock would be immediately eliminated by higher prices and the real money stock would be unchanged. It is more realistic to believe that the exchange rate can adjust rapidly, but that goods' prices (and money wages) are relatively sticky. As a result, the adjustment pressure will be reflected first in the exchange rate. It will jump up to *C* and then gradually fall to *B* as prices adjust over time. This reflects 'overshooting' of the exchange rate, since the initial devaluation is greater than that ultimately required. Further comment on this overshooting is required, since it is fully consistent with rational expectation formation.

What happens after a money supply increase if the price level does not immediately adjust? If domestic output is constrained not to rise, the pressure must be reflected in the domestic interest rate.

It will fall. This means that the interest parity condition 5.10 is violated. Since r^* is fixed, only x can now change to restore the equality. The value of r has fallen, so x must be negative if the domestic and foreign bonds are to have the same expected return. A negative x means an expected *appreciation* of the home currency. Long-run equilibrium requires a *depreciation* when compared to the initial point. These can only be reconciled if e immediately depreciates to a point from which it can be expected to appreciate during the adjustment of prices to the long-run equilibrium. This appreciation is just sufficient to compensate for the lower domestic interest rate. Hence, when the money stock increases the exchange rate depreciates too far and subsequently appreciates. This is what is meant by overshooting.

Notice that overshooting depends only on the price level being *relatively* sticky. There is no requirement of absolute fixity. The analysis will be more complex in reality to the extent that real income changes. It should be expected to change because at a point like C in figure 5.4 (indeed, any point off $p = e$), PPP does not hold so there will be expenditure shifts in favour of the economy with lower prices. In the case of domestic monetary expansion, the exchange rate depreciates too far so domestic goods become relatively cheap (temporarily). With a tightening of domestic monetary policy, the home currency over appreciates and domestic goods become relatively expensive.

We shall see that the over-appreciation of sterling in 1979 and 1980 is closely related to a subsequent decline in manufacturing output and employment. This is consistent with exchange rate overshooting caused by tight monetary policy. However, there is probably more to it than this. This is also the period when the maximum impact of North Sea oil was felt. Figure 5.5 shows the substantial swings in the sterling–dollar exchange rate. It also shows that there is no simple correlation between the exchange rate and the inflation differential, so that PPP is clearly violated. Indeed, in 1979 and 1980, when sterling appreciated against the dollar, inflation was consistently higher in the UK than in the US. This means that British goods were becoming more and more expensive relative to US goods. There will be further discussion of this point below.

Besides explaining specific episodes of exchange rate misalignment, this analysis also explains why exchange rates in general have

BALANCE OF PAYMENTS AND EXCHANGE RATES 105

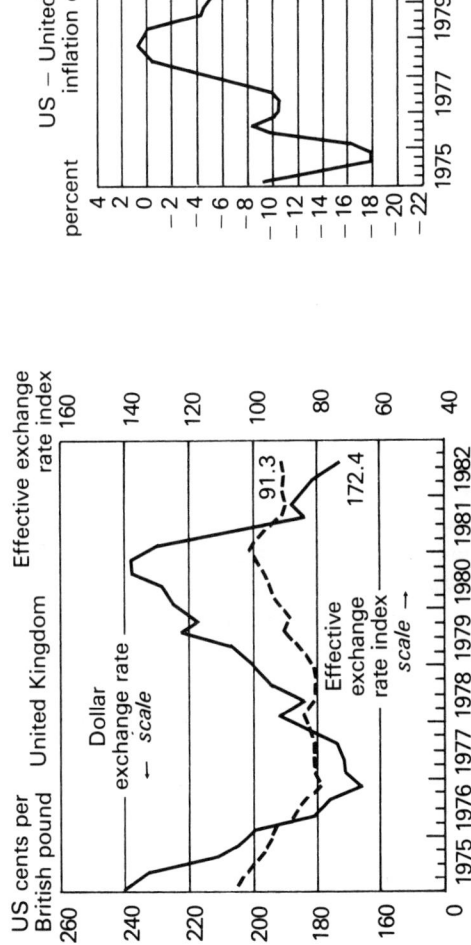

Source: 'International Economic Conditions', F.R.B. of St. Louis, 24 January 1983.

Figure 5.5

been so volatile. The system is recurrently being hit by disturbances or policy changes. If goods prices are sticky, the adjustment will be reflected in the exchange rate which can easily change from minute to minute. Thus, exchange rates should be expected to bounce about in response to 'news' in a way that is not possible in other markets. At the outset of floating many commentators argued that fluctuations would be reduced as the system settled down. This has not happened. Even (or perhaps, especially) in a model where actors hold rational expectations, there can be exchange rate overshooting so long as goods prices are *relatively* sticky in comparison to exchange rates.

Summary

In the 1950s and 1960s the balance of payments was the problem that dominated British macroeconomic policy. It was a problem precisely because the authorities had to finance deficits out of reserves while maintaining a fixed exchange rate. Keynesian and monetary approaches to the balance of payments offer different insights into the nature of the problem. Floating exchange rates provide a different policy environment. Excessive monetary expansion causes (and caused) currency depreciation and inflation. Excessive monetary contraction causes (and caused) currency appreciation (and unemployment, if prices and wages are sticky). Inflation and unemployment are the subject of the next chapter. Notice that the analysis of overshooting above offers a very plausible reason why fully-anticipated monetary policy will have real effects.

6

Inflation and Unemployment

Between 1951 and 1967 the rate of inflation in the UK never exceeded 6% per annum. In 1975 it was of the order of 25% per annum. It should be no surprise that economic policy of the 1970s was dominated by the problem of inflation. By early 1983 inflation was back below 6%. In contrast, unemployment drifted upwards during the 1970s. In 1974 it was 2.6% of the labour force. By 1979 it was at 5.1%. From early 1980 it accelerated dramatically. By early 1983 it had reached about 14%. Between the beginning of 1980 and the end of 1982 about 1.7 million jobs (net) disappeared in the UK. It is incumbent upon economists to offer some explanations of these dramatic events which have been variously blamed upon a decline in world demand, excessive unemployment benefits, monetarist deflation and many others. First, it is convenient to discuss the development of analytical models of the interaction of inflation and unemployment.

The Phillips Curve

One of the most famous relationships in macroeconomics is the inverse relationship between inflation and unemployment identified by A. W. Phillips (1958) and hence known as the Phillips curve. This relationship was, however, pointed out much earlier in the USA by Irving Fisher (1926). Further important supportive work on the Phillips curve was done by Lipsey (1960).

The problem Phillips posed for himself was how to explain the dynamic behaviour of a macro-model such as Model II when it was close to full employment. The textbook models had only real output changing at less than full employment, whereas at full employment only prices changed. Phillips focused particularly on the labour market and proposed that as the pressure of demand, as measured by unemployment, got greater and greater, the rate of increase of wages would rise. As a zero level of unemployment was approached the rate of increase of wages would approach infinity. Phillips showed that the evidence of nearly 100 years was consistent with the existence of a stable relationship as depicted in figure 6.1. The theoretical underpinnings were refined by Lipsey who worked

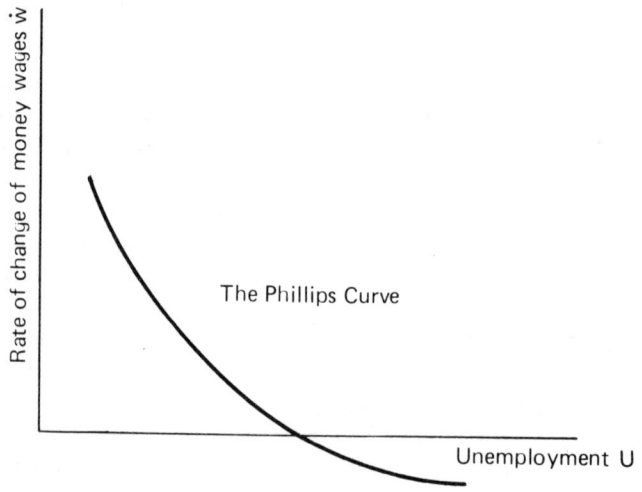

Figure 6.1

in terms of separate wage and price equations. Wages were determined by unemployment, and prices were determined by a markup on wages plus other costs. Followers often dropped this refinement and simply drew figure 6.1 with inflation,[1] $\dot{p}$, on the vertical axis instead of $\dot{w}$. It is now a commonplace to draw the Phillips curve as a relationship between p and U, and this practice will be continued below.

The Phillips curve was widely adopted by economists in the early 1960s as filling in a gap in the standard version of Model II. During this period it was generally accepted that inflation was mainly caused by demand factors, though even Phillips was fully aware that cost factors, especially import prices, *could* exert an independent influence on the price level. However, they had not often done so in the previous 100 years. The only serious support for the view that internal cost pressures could exert upward pressure on prices, independent of the level of demand, was offered by Hines (1964). Hines used the rate of change of union membership as an index of union pushfulness and claimed that this offered a significant improvement in the explanation of wage changes. Purdy and Zis (1973), however, provided a comprehensive critique of Hines' results.

After devaluation in 1967 the inflationary experience was considerably worse than previously, as Phillips himself would have predicted. Wages, however, lagged behind prices owing to the incomes policy of 1968-9 and also presumably because people did not know what to expect in terms of price rises. The resultant 'wage explosion' in 1969 was widely interpreted as proving the possibility of wage push independent of the level of demand. However, it can also be interpreted as a catch up of expectations. Laidler (1976) argues that over this period the country was merely reimporting the inflation it had previously been exporting.

Even if the data from the late 1960s could be made to fit with the simple Phillips curve, the data from the 1970s certainly could not. Indeed, the theoretical basis of the simple Phillips curve had been undermined independently by Phelps (1968) and Friedman (1968) long before events had made this reappraisal necessary. The Phelps–Friedman approach forms the basis of the model to be developed below.

An essential ingredient of the modified approach to the Phillips curve is the idea that unions bargain for real wages rather than nominal wages. Thus the Phillips curve has to be shifted up for each level of expected inflation. There is then a short-run trade off between inflation and unemployment for each *given* expected rate of inflation. It will be argued that there is more to the recent rise in unemployment than can be handled in the traditional framework.

Aggregate Demand and Supply

The major disagreement over the causes of inflation is often characterised as being between those who think it comes from aggregate demand and those who think it comes from the supply side of the economy. Most would agree that an expansion of the money stock is necessary to sustain a price level rise, but those who believe in cost-push usually argue that the money stock has to be expanded in the wake of inflation to avoid unemployment. Both lines of argument could be valid. The question is, what actually happened in any particular episode?

Let us first look at the price level and the level of output in terms of Model III. Following Gordon (1978) it is convenient to combine the two versions of Model III by a simple modification of the aggregate supply curve. For the short-run case where money illusion was assumed on the part of suppliers of labour, we assume that labour supply depends upon the expected price level p^e. Demand for labour on the other hand depends upon the actual price level. In the short run, while expectations lag behind reality, the aggregate supply curve will be upward sloping but it will shift leftward if expectations are revised upwards. In the long run expectations are correct so the long-run supply curve is vertical at the trend output level – sometimes called the 'natural' output level. In other words, the long-run supply curve shifts rightwards each period because of the underlying growth of the economy.

If we consider the initial position in figure 6.2 to be at point A then it is clear that a price level rise can be started by either a right-

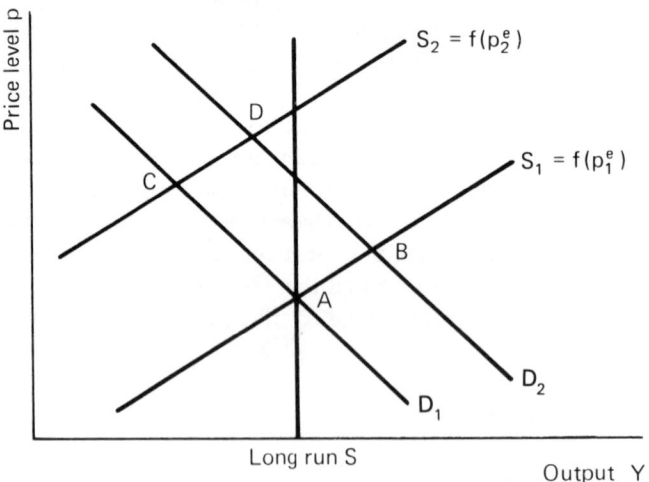

Figure 6.2

ward shift of aggregate demand D_1 or a leftward shift of aggregate supply. A cost-induced inflation would involve a supply side shift and the economy would move from A to C. A move to D would then follow if measures were taken to eliminate unemployment. Eventually the system would settle again at a higher price level on the long-run aggregate supply curve. A demand-induced inflation, however, would be caused by a shift of the demand curve to, say, D_2 so the economy would move from A to B. Expectations would then be revised so that S_1 would shift in the direction of S_2 and the economy would move to a point like D. Whether D is in this case to the left or right of long-run S does not matter – either is possible. The point is that a demand-induced inflation will move the economy through an anticlockwise arc initially. A supply-induced inflation will move it through a clockwise arc.

The picture in the UK in the early 1970s is extremely clear, as figure 6.3 shows, so long as it is appropriate to start the cycle in 1971. The end of 1971 marks the beginning of a major expansion of the money supply associated with competition and credit control, and March 1972 was the date of Mr Barber's famous expansionary budget. Hence a shift of demand moves the economy along a short-run supply curve, which incidentally appears to be fairly flat. From 1973 to 1975 it looks very much as if a leftward shift of the aggregate supply curve is moving the economy back up the aggregate demand curve, which is fairly steep. 1976 is almost due north of 1975, so there seems to be some reflation here plus a further shift left of the supply curve.

Notice that while the movement from 1973 to 1975 must involve a shift of the supply curve some such shift would be an essential part of the demand-induced story. The economy cannot stay at a point like B in figure 6.2 because it is beyond the long-run supply curve. Price expectations will necessarily shift the supply curve leftward sooner or later. It is quite likely that the oil price rise increased the shift of supply between 1973 and 1975, but it is important to realise that after the events of 1971–3 some such shift would have occurred anyway due to the behaviour of expectations.

The Expectations Augmented Phillips Curve

The above analysis is couched in terms of the price level and the

112 CONTROVERSIES IN MACROECONOMICS

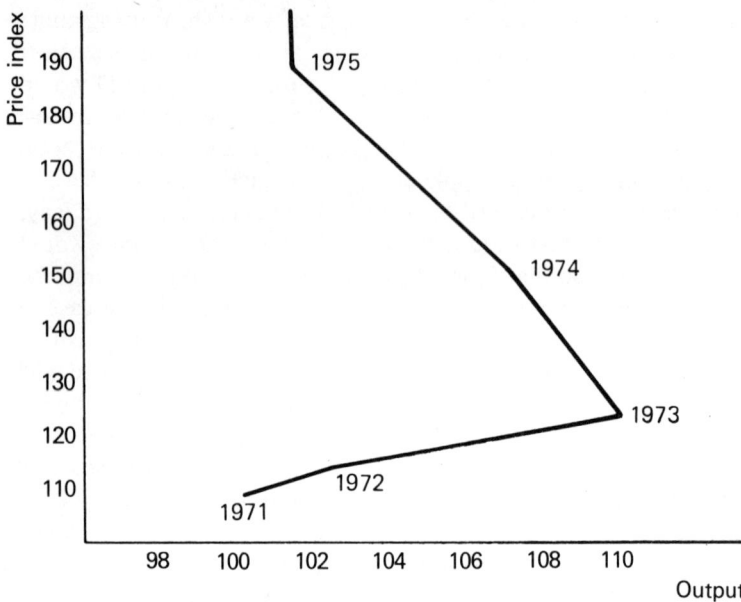

1970 = 100

	Price index all manufactured products	Output all industries
1971	109	100.3
1972	114.8	102.5
1973	123.2	109.9
1974	152	106.9
1975	188.7	101.5
1976	219.6	102

Figure 6.3 (Source: NIESR)

level of output. An analogous argument can be developed in the more familiar dimensions of inflation and unemployment. It was seen above that a single stable Phillips curve is incapable of reconciling the observation of both high inflation and high unemployment. However, once it is admitted that there is a new higher Phillips curve for each higher expected rate of inflation events become easy to explain.

Suppose curve PC_1 in figure 6.4 is the Phillips curve for zero expected inflation. If the level of unemployment is U^*, this expectation will be fulfilled and nothing need change. However, if

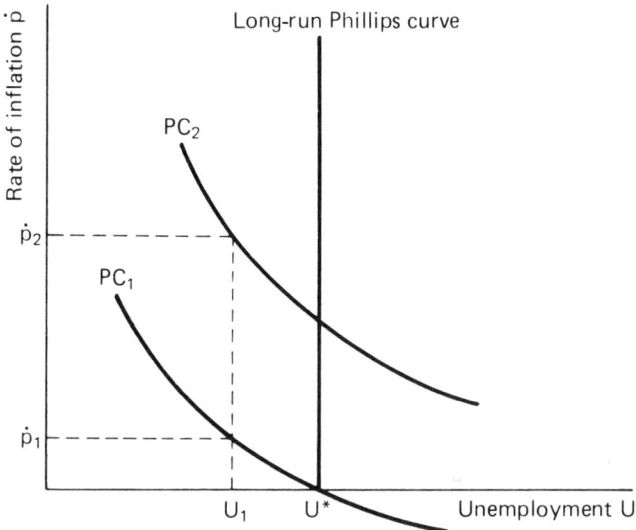

Figure 6.4

unemployment were U_1 inflation would be greater than zero at $\dot{p}_1$. Next period expectations would be revised upwards so there would be a higher Phillips curve, say PC_2, so again inflation would be higher than expected and, so long as unemployment stayed at U_1, inflation would accelerate. This is sometimes called the 'accelerationist' hypothesis as a result. The long-run Phillips curve traces out the point on each Phillips curve at which expectations will be fulfilled, so they are points of stable inflation. If the long run is defined as the period within which expectations are fulfilled, then the long-run Phillips curve is vertical *by definition*. The point on which it stands on the unemployment axis is known as the 'natural' rate of unemployment. This is thus exogenous to the inflation process but can be influenced by structural changes in the economy.

In order to explain what happens to the course of inflation and unemployment in reality it is necessary to add to this picture some statement about the growth of aggregate demand. There are really two separate relationships that can be identified between aggregate demand growth and inflation/unemployment. These are illustrated in figure 6.5. Let us assume for simplicity that there is no productivity growth, so that output is constant at the 'natural' level of unemployment. Whatever the rate of growth of aggregate monetary demand happens to be determines the long-run budget constraint of the economy. This tells us that the inflation rate (at a constant 'natural' output level) will be equal to the growth rate of aggregate demand. If aggregate demand in money terms is growing at 10% per annum the long-run budget constraint will be a horizontal line at a 10% inflation rate (or lower if the productivity assumption is changed).

There is no reason why the economy should be on the long-run budget constraint in each period. It will only be on LRBC when the economy is on the long-run aggregate supply curve, that is when output is not changing. Take the growth rate of *money* income as being exogenously fixed by policy. Then the short-run budget constraint that has to be satisfied is given by the fact that the rate of growth of money income is equal to the sum of the rate of growth of *real* income and the rate of inflation. So if there is some real income growth during the current period the inflation rate must be lower than the growth rate of money income. Let us also presume that there is a one to one relationship between real income (output) and unemployment. (A specific form of this relationship is known as Okun's Law). Higher output will be associated with lower unemployment. This means that we can express the short-run budget constraint as a relationship between inflation and unemployment.

To see what the short-run budget constraint must look like, start at point A in figure 6.5 on *LRBC*. If there is no real income growth, inflation will equal the growth of money income so the economy will stay at A. However, if there is real income growth in the current period, unemployment will fall and inflation will *necessarily* be less than the rate of growth of money income. The economy will go to a point like B. The short-run budget constraint is, therefore, positively sloped in inflation unemployment space, SBC_1.

Notice that point B is not sustainable for a second period. The move from A to B required real income growth and, therefore, a *fall* in unemployment from U_1 to U_2. If unemployment now stays at U_2, real income must be unchanged and so in the second period inflation must be equal to the rate of growth of money income – the economy would then be at C. This demonstrates that the short-run budget constraint for the second period must pass through C. In general, the SBC for a specific period cuts LRBC at the unemployment level achieved at the end of last period. This is because it depends upon the growth of real income when the base from which growth is measured is last year's level of real income. Each level of real income is associated with a specific level of unemployment.

Of course, if there is a change in aggregate demand policies, LRBC itself will shift and the exercise will start again at a point such as *A* on the new LRBC curve. The location of *A* is determined by the level of unemployment at the beginning of the period. However, in order to determine the actual course of inflation and unemployment we need to combine the budget constraints with the Phillips curves.

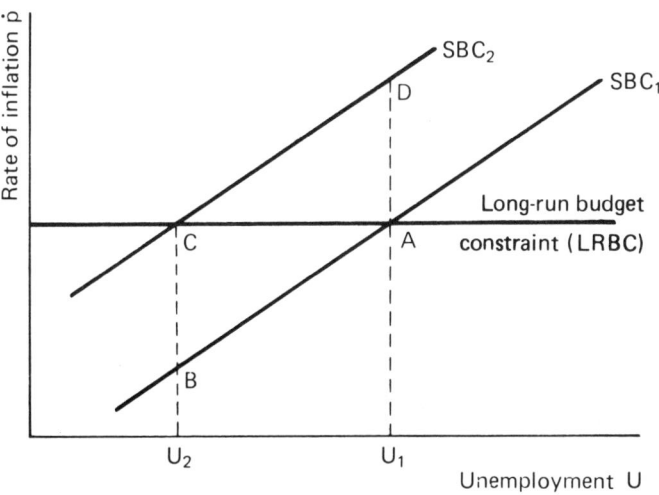

Figure 6.5 Budget constraints

Consider the course of inflation and unemployment that would occur if the economy were initially at the natural level of unemployment with zero inflation and zero growth of aggregate nominal demand. Now the growth rate of aggregate demand is raised to 10%. What happens? The long-run budget constraint becomes a horizontal line at the inflation rate of 10%, as depicted in figure 6.6. The new short-run budget constraint SBC_2 passes through the long-run budget constraint at the initial level of unemployment, i.e.

at G. The short-run Phillips curve is PC_1 so the economy moves from the initial position (U^*, $\dot{p}=0$) to A. Next period, the new short-run budget constraint will be SBC_3 and, if the short-run Phillips curve did not shift, the economy would go to B and then converge on C. However, expected inflation will now start to shift the short-run Phillips curve up to the right. If it now intersects SBC_3 at D the budget constraint will stay put for one period but the short-run Phillips curve will continue to move to the right.

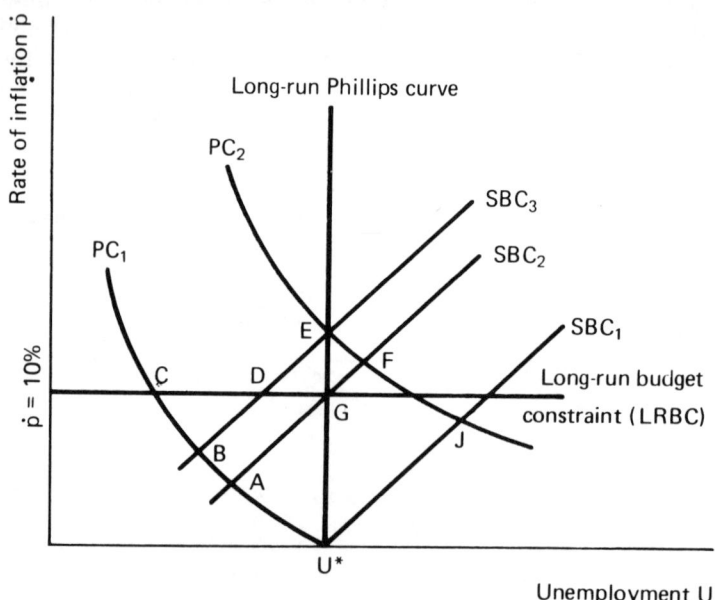

Figure 6.6

Once the intersection of PC and SBC is *above* the long-run budget constraint, the SBC curve will now start to shift back down to the right. And once the economy is *to the right* of the long-run Phillips curve, the PC curve will start to shift back down to the left. Thus from a point such as E which is on PC_2 and SBC_3 we move to F on PC_2 and SBC_2. From F both the SBC curve and the PC curve will shift down, so the next position could well be southeast of G. Clearly, the economy will home into the long-run equilibrium point G in a clockwise cycle, presuming, that is, that the expectations feedback is reasonably stable, so that the economy does not explode.

It is important to notice that, while we have conducted the simplest possible experiment of raising demand growth from zero to 10%, we have discovered a pattern of response which includes periods of rising inflation and rising unemployment, falling inflation and rising unemployment, as well as rising inflation and falling unemployment. The economy has moved through a clockwise convergent cycle from the initial position through A, D, E and F, and eventually to G.

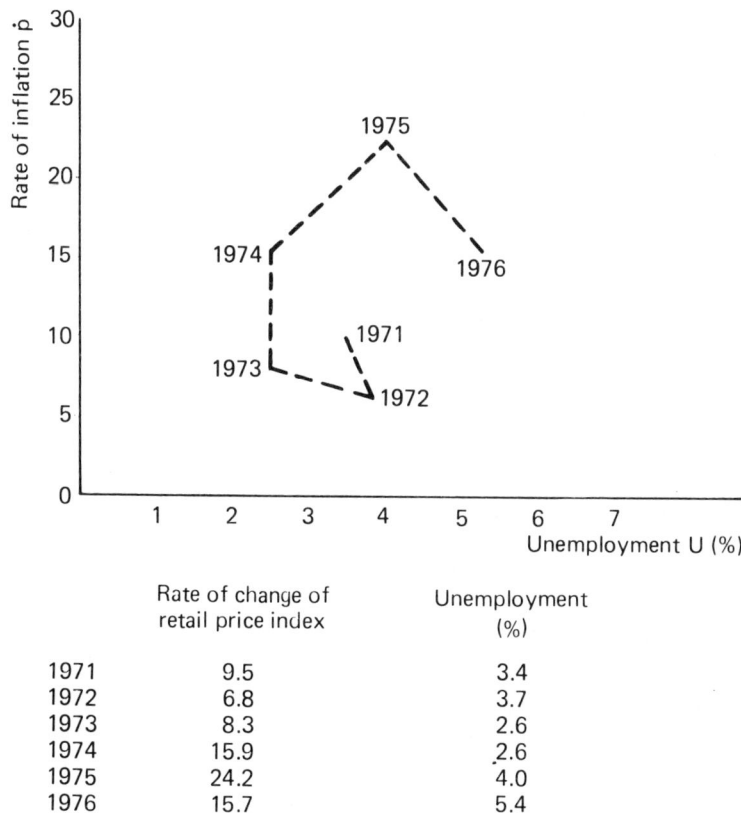

	Rate of change of retail price index	Unemployment (%)
1971	9.5	3.4
1972	6.8	3.7
1973	8.3	2.6
1974	15.9	2.6
1975	24.2	4.0
1976	15.7	5.4

Figure 6.7 (Source: NIESR)

Figure 6.7 plots the actual course of the UK economy during its inflation cycle of 1971-6. The movement from 1971 to 1972 can be regarded as the tail of the previous cycle. From 1972 there is a clear clockwise cycle which is entirely consistent with a demand-induced inflation as above. Specific factors such as the oil price rise and incomes policies will no doubt have an influence on the numerical size of various shifts. But it is hard to see how these specific factors could explain the pattern as a whole. For example, if the 1973 oil crisis had struck at the initial position in figure 6.6 and the authorities had maintained the level of domestic demand constant, the economy would initially have moved northeast to a point like J.

On the basis of figure 6.7 the natural rate of unemployment looks to be of the order of 3 or 4%. Indeed Sumner (1978) estimated it at 3.2% for this period and Batchelor and Sheriff (1980) estimate the 'equilibrium' level for this period to be 4%. As a result of this analysis one would have concluded that the economy should home-in on an unemployment rate of 3-4% at some stable inflation rate. The latter should have been reasonably low given the adoption of fairly restrictive aggregate demand policies in late 1976. This, of course, did not happen. The above analysis has been deliberately retained from the first edition of this book because it is instructive about the conventional wisdom of the time. The policies pursued by both the Labour Government of James Callaghan after 1976 and the Conservative Government of Margaret Thatcher after its election in May 1979 should have had a better effect on the British economy. Subscribers to the above view of the world should not have viewed their policies with total disfavour. It should have been possible to have unemployment in the region of 4%, with inflation below 10% by 1980.

The Economics of 1978-1982

As figure 6.8 graphically demonstrates, the economy did not home-in on 4% unemployment. Rather, unemployment accelerated dramatically from early 1980 to reach a level of nearly 14% in early 1983. It is true that inflation had also come down to about 5% by early 1983, but on the basis of previous patterns this should have been possible at very much higher levels of employment. The rise in inflation from 1978 to 1980 may be explainable in terms of a number of temporary factors such as the 1979 oil price rise and the

INFLATION AND UNEMPLOYMENT 119

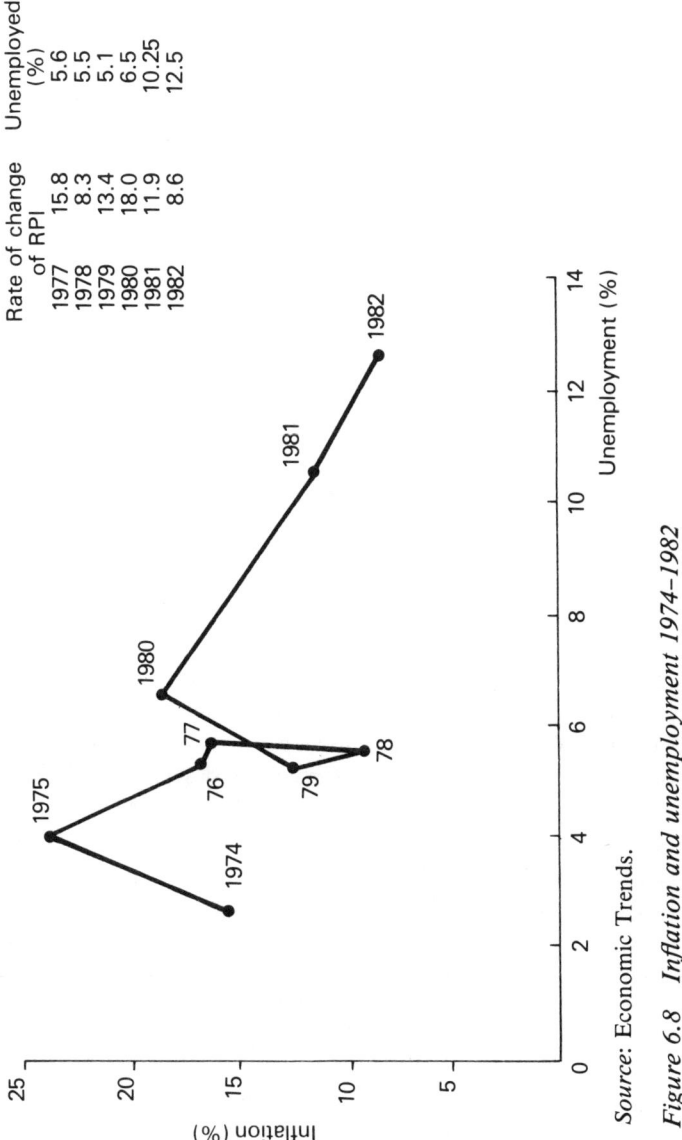

Source: Economic Trends.

Figure 6.8 Inflation and unemployment 1974–1982

increase in VAT resulting from the June 1979 Budget. The real problem, however, is to explain the massive rise in unemployment.

There are a number of false trails which, for completeness, deserve a mention but little more. One is that high unemployment benefits shifted the natural rate of unemployment so that millions of workers now 'chose' to be out of work, the utility of not working being greater than that in work. This explanation is preposterous. It is quite likely that the level of unemployment benefits has some marginal effect on the level of measured unemployment. But it is absurd to suggest that this can explain job losses in Britain in recent years.

Another suggestion is that Britain suffered from a decline in world trade. There is a modicum of truth to this, but it can explain only a tiny fraction of the problem. World trade in manufactures, in fact, continued to grow in volume terms until some time in the middle of 1981. Indeed, British exports of manufactures in volume terms were virtually constant in the four years 1977-80, and declined by only about 4% in 1981 to then level-off for 1982. The events of importance for employment precede this drop in exports by between one and two years.

A third explanation which has more widespread support is that the British economy suffered a massive deflation ('Monetarist') of domestic aggregate demand through cutbacks of domestic expenditures. Perhaps surprisingly, this is also hard to sustain. Table 6.1 shows the breakdown of expenditures in constant (1975) prices. The two major categories of spending – personal consumption and government current expenditure on goods and services – have a rising trend throughout the period. Investment declines but only latterly, and there is a running down in the last two years of the stocks built up in the 1976-9 period.

It could be argued that this shows that the 'transmission mechanism' is through high real interest rates causing a fall in investment and a run down of stocks. This is certainly contributory, but it is not the main event. Notice that the volume of demand in 1981 is about the same as in 1978 and yet between those two dates unemployment has more than doubled. Notice also that the run down of stocks in 1980 and 1981 was still less than the build up in the previous four years. This suggests that we look to these earlier years and ask why it was that stocks of unsold goods were building up. Domestic consumption was rising consistently and yet

Table 6.1 Expenditures (£M 1975 prices)

Year	Total	Personal consumption	Government current expenditure	Investment	Change in stocks
1974	136,670	65,049	21,774	20,562	1,401
1975	133,771	64,652	22,950	20,408	−1,436
1976	138,778	64,707	23,178	20,640	658
1977	140,497	64,517	22,951	20,139	1,382
1978	145,748	68,227	23,438	20,845	1,146
1979	151,200	71,599	23,866	21,039	1,782
1980	147,806	71,550	24,311	20,443	−1,555
1981	145,409	71,871	24,306	18,774	−1,871

Source: Economic Trends.

domestic manufacturers were consistently producing more than they could sell. How can these apparent inconsistencies be reconciled?

The answer turns out to be remarkably simple. It is that there was a substantial *shift* of domestic demand away from domestic manufactured goods towards imported manufactured goods. This

Table 6.2

	Year	Imports Fuels	Imports Manufactures	Exports Fuels	Exports Manufactures
	1973	131	101	117	98
	1974	123	107	109	103
	1975	100	100	100	100
	1976	100	109	120	109
	1977	83	119	165	117
	1978	80	133	209	116
	1979	78	153	277	116
	1980	66	151	290	117
	1981	54	153	357	112
	1982	49	166	389	112
Value	1975	4,316	12,567	827	16,033
	1982	7,460	37,093	11,193	37,318

(Volume, 1975 = 100)

Source: NIESR.

is graphically illustrated by table 6.2. There was a 66% increase in the volume of imports of manufactures between 1975 and 1982, with the bulk of the rise coming before the end of 1979. Notice that manufactured imports and exports move together until after 1977 when exports level off and imports accelerate. The switch does not produce an immediate decline in production by domestic industry. Rather, they build up stocks of unsold products, as we have seen. The production pattern changes dramatically after 1979. Between late 1979 and the end of 1980 there is a massive fall in industrial production of the order of 15%. This fall is largely over by 1981, though the annual average figures look like they continue to fall (the average index for 1980 is higher than the index at the end of the year). This massive fall in production is clearly correlated with the period of major rise in unemployment and precedes it by some months. Production starts to dive in late 1979 and unemployment starts to accelerate in early 1980.

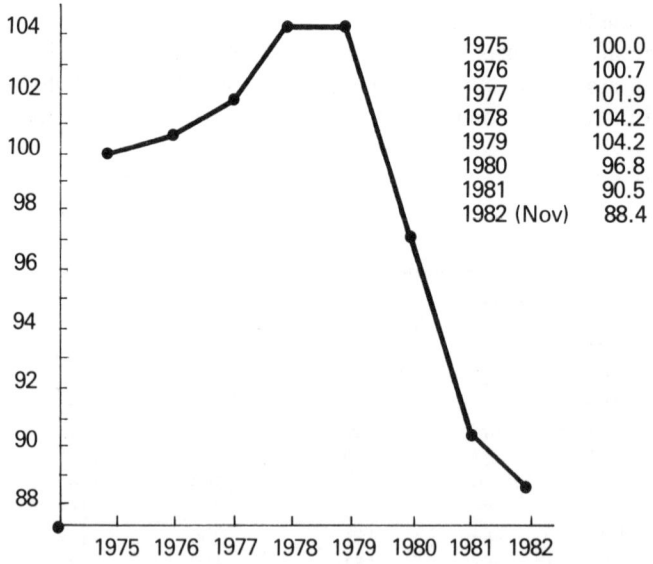

Source: Economic Trends.

Figure 6.9   Index of industrial production (excluding oil and gas)

The speed of this adjustment presumably owes something to high real interest rates, but it should be clear by now that this is not the cause. There had been over-production for some years. The problem was that domestic firms had, over successive years, lost their grip on the home market. There was no compensating expansion of exports. This increase of import penetration was not due to an upsurge of incompetence on the part of domestic producers. Rather, the explanation is to be found in the fact that this is the period of maximum expansion of North Sea oil production. Table 6.2 shows the steady decline of fuel imports and rise in fuel exports. This is associated with a substantial appreciation of sterling as we saw in Chapter 5. This appreciation of sterling, remarkably, had only a minor effect on the volume of manufactured exports, but it had a substantial effect on imports of manufactures. Domestic producers were squeezed out of the home market.

This is the cause of the rise in unemployment. Something like 1½ million jobs were lost in manufacturing industry between 1979 and 1982. Certainly monetary policies contributed to the problem by increasing the over-appreciation of sterling. However, a major contributory factor must be the changing oil balance of this period. Total imports and exports move more or less in line when oil is included. This suggests that the exchange rate moves to clear the current account in the long run as implied by the analysis of Chapter 5, though at times it may have moved too far. There is further discussion of the analytics of this problem in Chapter 9 below.

There is one further point worth making at this stage. This is that if the above argument is correct, it throws some light on the argument made in some circles that excessive capital outflows are causally related to domestic job losses. We have seen that job losses were due to an appreciation of sterling which made domestic manufactures relatively expensive. In so far as some of this appreciation was exchange rate overshooting of the type discussed in Chapter 5 above, the appropriate policy would have been to *encourage* capital outflows and discourage inflows. It does not make any sense at all to argue that sterling was over-valued and that capital outflows were excessive. They are inconsistent statements. In reality, what is hard to explain is why private sector investment in Britain held up so well in this period. In any event, there is no direct relationship between external financial flows and domestic real investment.

The implications of the above argument for traditional macroeconomic management of the economy are far from clear. At the time of writing some are arguing that the solution to the unemployment problem is a substantial reflation of aggregate demand. Yet we have seen that the problem was not caused by a deficiency of domestic spending. The success of any reflation would depend on the extent to which it could *lower* the relative price of British manufactures. The important point to notice, however, is that traditional macroeconomics – Keynesian, Monetarist or New Classical – is not much help. The central issue is how to adjust to a change in the structure of the productive sector of the economy. The expansion of a non-labour intensive sector has 'crowded out' the relatively labour intensive manufacturing sector. To what extent has there been 'overshooting' in the adjustment process? Has the 'natural rate' of unemployment permanently shifted? Is the 'natural rate' still a relevant concept? Will the economy adjust automatically to solve these problems or is there some policy that would help? These are some of the important questions, but macroeconomics is not well placed to answer them. Macroeconomics of all flavours has taken the supply structure of the economy to be homogeneous and stable. For Britain in recent years these are not reasonable assumptions. Policy solutions based on these traditional approaches should, therefore, be viewed with suspicion.

Modelling Labour Markets

The workings of the labour market have always been of interest to economists because the presence of unemployment has wider social and political implications which would not arise if there was, for example, an excess supply of timber. In most cases it is clear that it is inappropriate to analyse the labour market as if it were an auction market in which prices adjust continuously to equate demand and supply. In the short run at least, the labour market is better modelled as a Hicksian 'fix-price' market, or what Okun (1981) calls a 'customer' market. The latter is an instructive term because it points to the fact that employers have a relationship with their employees which is mutually advantageous. This relationship would be hard to sustain if employers changed wage rates arbitrarily each day in response to the availability of labour.

A formal literature has now developed which analyses this

'implicit contract' between employers and workers. (The original ideas are due to Azariadis 1975 and Baily 1974. For a recent contribution see Grossman and Hart 1981.) If workers are averse to risk and firms are risk neutral it is possible to show that an arrangement satisfactory to both will involve stable wage rates with firms absorbing demand fluctuation to some degree. By this method it is possible to explain sticky wages as a characteristic of an 'optimal' contract. However, the full implications of this line of analysis for macroeconomics are still being pursued. This is an area in which further work remains to be done.

Incomes Policies

The recent increase in unemployment has caused some resurgence of interest in incomes policies as a way of holding down wages and prices during a reflation of aggregate demand. Incomes policies have been tried from time to time in the UK, but they are generally viewed with scepticism by professional economists.

The academic objection to incomes policy is usually based upon three propositions. The first is that *independent* wage-push is not the cause of inflation and so an incomes policy must eventually be frustrated because it does not tackle the root cause of the problem. This leads to the second point which is that while an incomes policy can have no long-run effect, it will work in holding down wages in some areas, and so there will be distortions introduced in the allocation of labour. The economy will thus be less efficient. Finally, and perhaps strongest of all, is the point that it has proved extremely difficult to demonstrate that incomes policies have had any significant effect at all in the UK in the last 25 years. Parkin, Sumner and Jones (1972), for example, in their survey of the evidence on this subject, conclude that:

> . . . On the basis of our present knowledge, it is possible to say that, with the exception of the immediate post-war experiment, incomes policy apparently has little effect either on the wage determination process or on the average rate of wage inflation . . . (p. 13)
> . . . The existing evidence indicates that incomes policies have had no identifiable effect on the price equation . . . (p. 25.)

How then might an incomes policy work in the context of the model in figure 6.6? It should be clear that the long-run position of the economy depends only upon the long-run budget constraint and upon the natural rate of unemployment. The long-run budget constraint depends entirely upon the policy-determined growth of monetary demand. So incomes policy could not influence the long-run inflation rate in this model. However, it could influence the short-run course of the economy *if and only if* it succeeds in lowering inflationary expectations. In this case the short-run Phillips curve would shift down to the left. For a given short-run budget constraint inflation would be lower and employment would be higher than otherwise. If this could be achieved, then, even if the long-run inflation rate was unchanged, a higher average level of output and lower average unemployment could be attained. This would undoubtedly be preferable to the situation in which there was no incomes policy.

The problem with an incomes policy is that even if the initial effect is favourable, the belief that the policy is ending can have an equally adverse effect or even worse. The expectation of the collapse of an incomes policy would shift the short-run Phillips curve up to the right, thus making inflation and unemployment worse. Many economists believe that this is exactly what happens. A short-run benefit is fairly quickly offset by an equal deterioration. Henry and Ormerod (1978), for example, conclude that:

> ... Whilst some incomes policies have reduced the rate of wage inflation during the period in which they operated, this reduction has only been temporary. Wage increases in the period immediately following the ending of the policies were higher than they would otherwise have been, and these increases match losses incurred during the operation of the incomes policy. (p. 39.)

Thus while it is logically possible that incomes policies could improve the dynamic path towards *any* long-run inflation rate, there is no evidence that they have done so in the recent past. Any short-run benefit in terms of higher employment and lower inflation is subsequently offset by higher inflation and lower employment as the policy breaks down.

There are two possible stories about this breakdown. The first is the catching up of expectations that has been mentioned above. The second gives a critical role to the public sector. It is argued that incomes policies have their greatest impact on public sector wages since the government is in effect itself the employer, whereas private sector employers can get around the policy if market conditions demand. As time passes the public sector employees notice that their wages are falling behind comparable private sector groups and demand 'pay comparability'. This leads to substantial public sector 'catch up' awards which effectively herald the end of the incomes policy. In 1979 the Labour Government even went so far as to set up a Public Sector Comparability Commission to deal with the multiplicity of public sector groups who felt that they had suffered under successive phases of incomes policies.

This points to the existence of two separate problems in this area. The first is how to make incomes policies more widely effective and other than in the short run. The answer to this is that it is probably not worth trying, since the administrative and distortionary costs would seem to be prohibitive in peace time. The second problem is how to determine public sector wages. The larger is the public sector share of employment the more inappropriate it becomes to set public sector wages by comparison with the private sector. In the end there could be just one man left in the private sector whose wages determine those for the rest of the economy! A more coherent public sector wages policy is required which is made consistent with other aspects of policy such as employment and public expenditure targets and bears a sensible relationship to the underlying growth pattern of the real economy. Neither the adoption or abandonment of incomes policies obviates the need for a sensible policy towards public sector pay.

A new form of incomes policy has recently been advocated in the UK (Layard 1982). This was first suggested in the US under the name 'tax based incomes policy', but in the UK it has come to be known as the 'inflation tax.' The idea is simply that a tax should be imposed on firms which pay wage rises in excess of some norm. Proponents of this scheme in the UK have not used short-run arguments, but rather have claimed that it will reduce the natural rate of unemployment. It may seem strange that a tax on wages could increase equilibrium employment. But the argument depends upon the tax reducing the monopoly power of unions and thereby lowering the equilibrium real wage. It is far from clear how general this result is, so again it should be treated with caution.

There are a number of practical objections to the inflation tax. It is hard to administer. Would it not be a tax on fast growth firms which had good reason to offer higher wages as a way of attracting labour? Real wage increases justified by productivity should be encouraged, not discouraged, and, of course, they have nothing to do with inflation. Most importantly, however, as has been argued above, the real problem is wage determination in the public sector. The inflation tax would do nothing for this.

Summary

Britain is a small economy in a big world. Some of its economic history is explained by world developments alone. The inflation of the mid-1970s and the unemployment of the early 1980s were both worse than could be blamed upon developments in the world economy. The former is largely explained by the excessive fiscal and monetary expansion of the 1971–3 period. The latter results from an over-appreciation of sterling caused by a combination of North Sea oil and tight monetary policies. The relevance of the 'natural rate' framework for the analysis of unemployment in the 1980s is questioned.

Note

1 Notice the confusion of notation. It is conventional now to use $\dot{p} = dp/dt$. The rate of inflation should therefore be $\dot{p}/p$. However, $\dot{p}$ is used for convenience.

7
Crowding Out

One of the central tenets of Political Monetarism, or the new conservative macroeconomics, is that the excessive growth of 'government' has been harmful to economic performance. The public sector is alleged to utilise resources inefficiently, and the taxes necessary to pay for public services are claimed to be a disincentive to productive effort. The purpose of this chapter is to discuss some of the macroeconomic aspects of this issue. The broader question of government versus the market is surveyed in Alt and Chrystal (1983).

Within the Keynesian paradigm an increase in government expenditure would increase the level of national income by some multiple of the initial expenditure, through the multiplier process. Some resources would thus be acquired by the public sector, but the resulting income of the private sector would be even greater than it was before. This picture may be correct for the situation of a deep depression, but it would not seem to characterise the behaviour of modern economies closer to the full employment level of output. Crowding out can be said to occur when an increase in government expenditure of, say, £100m leads to an increase in national income of less than £100m. In other words, crowding out is associated with the existence of a multiplier effect of less than unity. This is so called because it means that, as a result of resources being diverted into the public sector, the private sector is left with fewer resources than it had before. Super-crowding out arises when the multiplier is negative. Even if the multiplier is greater than unity there may be 'partial' crowding out in some areas. For example, investment may fall even if consumption has risen by a greater amount.

It is important to realise that this attitude to state intervention is not new. Rather it is as old as economics itself. The Keynesian view is the misfit, though this does not make it wrong. Spencer and Yohe (1970), for example, point out that even Adam Smith believed that government spending financed by borrowing involved '... the destruction of some capital which had before existed in the country, by the perversion of some portion of the annual produce which had before been destined for the maintenance of productive labour, towards that of unproductive labour' (*Wealth of Nations*, 1937 edn, p. 878). Spencer and Yohe (p. 15) also refer to Hawtrey's evidence to the Macmillan Committee in 1930: 'Hawtrey stated that whether the spending came out of taxes or loans from savings, the increased governmental expenditures would merely replace private expenditures.'

The recent resurgence of a belief in crowding out is clearly associated with the monetarist critique, but it did not flow directly from the work of Friedman himself.[1] Rather, the main impetus came from the work of Anderson and Jordan (1968). They ran a reduced form regression of money national income on current and lagged values of government expenditure and current and lagged values of the money stock. The results indicated that while the impact effect of expenditure was positive this was soon offset by negative effects, so that, '... A change in Federal spending financed by either borrowing or taxes has only a negligible effect on GNP over a period of about a year' (Carlson and Spencer 1975, p. 3). Monetary expansion, on the other hand, had a positive cumulative effect. For recent estimates of the 'St. Louis equation' see Batten and Hafer (1983).

It is fair to record that the Anderson and Jordan result has been widely discredited. This is partly due to the failure of their equation on more recent data. But more important is the theoretical argument of Goldfeld and Blinder (1972) who point to the inaccuracy of reduced-form techniques when the government reacts systematically to the state of the economy. An intuitive explanation of the Goldfeld–Blinder point is presented by Chrystal and Alt (1979). Basically, if fiscal stabilisation policy is designed to offset the effects of fluctuations in an exogenous variable, there need be no correlation between income and the budget deficit even if fiscal policy is working *perfectly* as a stabiliser.[2]

By now, of course, the intellectual bandwagon of crowding out is rolling so fast that it matters not whether what started it is correct. What is important for present purposes, however, is to understand how crowding out could occur in the context of the macro-models that have been used above. The reader can then form his own view about their relevance to reality.

A further important point to be aware of before proceeding is that the crowding out issue is often regarded as being identical to the question of the effects of the government budget constraint. The latter arises because if the government runs a budget deficit this must be financed either by money printing, borrowing or raising taxes. This restriction has often been ignored in the past, as indeed it is in all three textbook models above. We shall see below that crowding out could occur even without a government budget equation but that, once the government's financing requirement is taken into account, crowding out becomes so much more likely as to be highly probable, except when there is considerable slack in the economy.

The IS-LM Classical Case

It was seen in Chapter 3 that one common interpretation of both the monetarist and the classical case arises if the demand for money is strictly proportional to income. The effect of this in terms of Model II is that the LM curve becomes vertical. This is illustrated in figure 7.1 where LM_c is the relevant curve. A shift of the IS curve from IS_1 to IS_2 caused by an increase in government expenditure in Model I (The Keynesian expenditure system) would have caused an increase in income from Y_0 to Y_1. But with a vertical LM curve there can be no increase in income. Rather, the interest rate rises to r_2 until there has been a reduction in private investment equal to the initial rise in government expenditure. Even if the LM curve was upward sloping, as it clearly is in reality, there would still be *some* partial crowding out of private investment say on LM_1 at an interest rate of r_1. But the rise in income from Y_0 to Y_2 *could* represent a multiplier in excess of unity.

132 CONTROVERSIES IN MACROECONOMICS

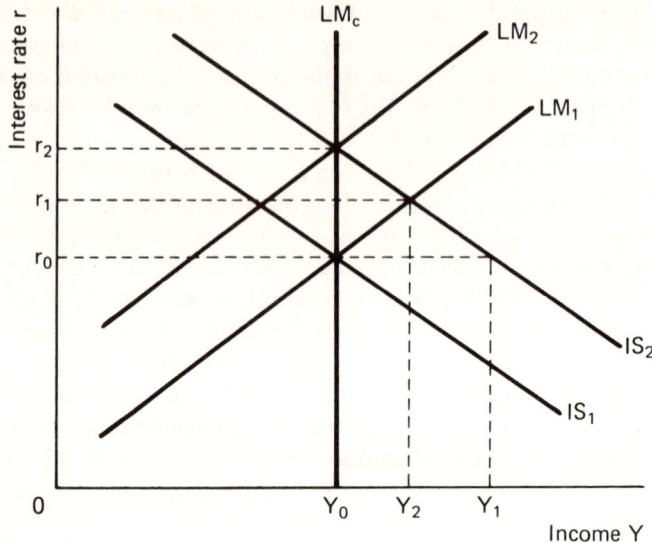

Figure 7.1

Other Model II Possibilities

A number of other cases are listed by Carlson and Spencer (1975) and it is convenient to present these among others, though some of them would seem a bit unlikely.

1. The Expectations Effect

At one point in the 'General Theory' Keynes himself suggested that a government expenditure programme could, in 'the confused psychology which often prevails', have an adverse effect on confidence. This could cause either an offsetting reduction in private investment or an upward shift in the LM curve. Both could cause crowding out with respect to income and the latter would involve a higher interest rate. This case seems unlikely to be of general importance, though it may apply in certain unusual circumstances.

2. Horizontal IS Curve

If investment were perfectly elastic with respect to the interest rate, the IS curve would be horizontal and fiscal policy would not shift it. Since national income is fixed by the LM curve, a rise in government expenditure would be exactly offset by a reduction in private expenditures. This is a pathological case which can be immediately dismissed as unreasonable.

3. Direct Substitution Effects

There may be some areas in which government expenditures provide services which the private sector would otherwise buy for themselves. Thus it is possible that there is some direct substitutability between state and private expenditures, but it is not very likely that this substitutability is of major significance at the margin.

4. Full Employment Price Level Effect

It should go without saying that if the initial position of the economy is at full employment, say at $r_0 Y_0$ in figure 7.1, there can be no increase in income. A shift in the IS curve to IS_2 will lead to a price level rise which will shift the LM curve to LM_2. Government expenditure will necessarily have a multiplier effect of zero, and again it will lead to an equal reduction in private investment.

5. Financing Effect – The Budget Restriction

The case which has been emphasised by Friedman relies upon the fact that sales of debt by the government will reinforce the negative feedback already noted in Model II. Consider the initial position in figure 7.1 at $r_0 Y_0$ on IS_1 and LM_1. An increase in government expenditure shifts the IS curve to IS_2 and the economy to $r_1 Y_2$. This rise in the interest rate is due to the increased transactions demand for money coupled with a fixed money supply. The rise in the budget deficit will have to be financed by sales of government debt which will put further upward pressure on interest rates. This upward pressure will be cumulative, so long as the deficit persists, whereas the initial multiplier is of a once-and-for-all nature. Thus any positive initial effect on income will eventually be offset by the negative cumulative effect of debt sales on private investment expenditures.

6. Balanced Budget Multiplier

Even in Model I, if an increase in government expenditure is financed by raising income taxes, the so-called balanced budget multiplier would be equal to unity. In Model II, however, since there is some rise in income with a fixed money supply, interest rates will have to rise. There will be some reduction in private investment and so the balanced budget multiplier becomes less than unity. Thus an increase in government expenditure financed by raising taxes will almost certainly involve some crowding out.

Crowding Out in Model III

It should be clear that, apart from case 4 above where output is fixed, if we add a supply side to the model, crowding out will be even more likely to occur. Consider, for example, the version of Model III outlined in Chapter 6. This is pictured in figure 7.2. The short-run aggregate supply curve AS_s is upward sloping because labour supply depends upon expected prices, whereas demand for

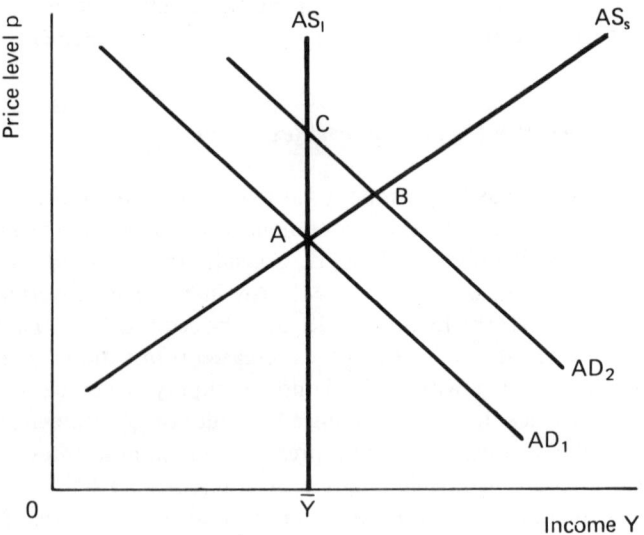

Figure 7.2

labour depends upon actual prices. There is a rise in output in the short run because expectations lag behind actuality and so there is a temporary fall in the real wage. More labour is employed and more output produced.

An initial increase in government expenditure would move the economy from A to B (ignoring the government budget constraint). However, over time price expectations will catch up with reality and, as they do, the short-run aggregate supply curve will shift up to the left. Eventually the economy will settle again at C where output is on the long-run aggregate supply curve. All the increase in government expenditure will have crowded out private expenditures of an equal amount. Largely it will be private investment crowded out since the fall in the real money stock will raise interest rates. Thus the story we are left with from this model is that crowding out is quite likely in the long run but there may be a short period during which government expenditure leads to income increases through the multiplier process. Only if the economy could be shown to start off well to the left of the AS_1 curve, and not to be there because of an inflation cycle, could we argue that there was a chance that there would be no long-run crowding out.

An additional factor which could increase the likelihood of *short-run* crowding out would be if price expectations are formed 'rationally', in the sense defined in Chapter 4. Above it has implicitly been assumed that price expectations are formed as a revision from the prediction error made last time. If, however, all actors understand the model and realise that the expansion of government expenditure is going to raise prices, it could be that there will be no short-run output gain at all. Rather, the AS_s curve will shift up rapidly and the economy will go straight from A to C. This is the source of the argument that only unanticipated policy changes will have any real effects.

The remaining question concerns the position of the long-run supply curve. It has been argued that this will be positioned at the 'natural' level of output. This is basically determined from year to year by the underlying growth trend of the economy. It would seem from the above analysis that the only chance of long-run crowding out *not* occurring is if rises in government expenditure can somehow increase the underlying growth potential of the economy. This is certainly possible in principle but the most vociferous commentators on this issue believe that exactly the opposite will occur.

Brunner and Meltzer (1976, p. 769), for example, argue that:

> Reduction in the output of the private sector could, in principle, be offset by the increased output of the public sector . . . It does not happen. Instead, there are loans or subsidies to enterprises that earn no profit or suffer large losses. Private saving is directed, in this case, toward enterprises that often do not earn rates of return equal to the interest on the bonds issued to finance the government budget deficit. Or, investment is used to increase 'prestige' as in the case of Concorde, national airlines, steamship lines and other enterprises that operate at negative rates of return. These enterprises direct material, skilled labour, and capital toward less productive uses than the private output that is crowded out. The list of such enterprises can be expanded by every knowledgeable reader.
>
> Absorption of labour by the government does not substitute public output for private output of equivalent value. Much public employment has the opposite effect. Complex rules and regulations absorb the time of civil servants and create demands in the private sector for lawyers, accountants, negotiators and clerks to keep abreast of the rules, to fill out the forms and hopefully to obtain more favourable interpretations than competitors have obtained.
>
> Employment is generated by this process, but much of the output produced by the employees has little value to society. More efficient output is crowded out, replaced by records, completed forms and administrative decrees that in the aggregate subtract more than they add to wealth and to welfare.

We shall return to this question a little later in the chapter.

Crowding out in the Treasury Model

One way of testing for the presence of crowding out is to use estimated econometric forecasting models to simulate the effects of various policy changes. Lewis and Ormerod (1979) present the results of simulations on the Treasury and National Institute forecasting models (as of March 1978). A selection of these results will be considered for the Treasury model alone. Before doing this it is worth recalling the criticisms of this procedure made by Robert Lucas (see Chapter 4). Such exercises require the structural model of the economy to be policy invariant. There is no reason to believe that this is so. As a result, the safest conclusion is that these simulations tell us a lot about the properties of the model in question but, perhaps, not very much about the properties of the economy itself.

Multiplier Effect on Real GDP of Various Policies in the Treasury Model

Table 7.1 reports the multiplier effects produced in the Treasury model as a result of a number of different initial changes. The first simulation is for a rise of government consumption of £100m, holding interest rates, exchange rate and earnings fixed. This is the nearest thing possible in the model to the idea of the Keynesian multiplier. What is most surprising is that even without interest rate or price level feedbacks and with no supply side and no budget constraint in the model, the multiplier turns out to be only unity. Allowance for any of these omitted factors would obviously introduce some crowding out. The second simulation proves this because, for the same experiment but with earnings and the exchange rate endogenised, the eventual multiplier rate is lowered to 0.8.

Table 7.1 Multipliers in Treasury Model

	\multicolumn{6}{c}{Approximate multiplier after number of years}
	1	2	3	4	5	6
1. Government consumption + £100m; interest rate, earnings, exchange rate fixed.	1.1	1.05	1.0	1.0	1.0	1.0
2. Government consumption + £100m; interest rate fixed, earnings endogenous, floating exchange rate.	1.1	1.04	0.9	0.8	0.8	0.8
3. Income tax reduced £100m; interest rates fixed, earnings endogenous, floating exchange rate.	0.4	0.55	0.9	1.15	1.38	1.4
4. Balanced budget: increase of taxes and government expenditure of £100m; interest rate fixed, earnings endogenous, exchange rate floating.	0.75	0.4	0	−0.4	−0.58	−0.6

The difference in effect achieved by lowering income tax rather than raising expenditure is shown in simulation 3. Here it takes six years to build up to the full multiplier effect of 1.4, whereas the first simulation reached the ultimate value of 1 within a couple of years. Finally, simulation 4 shows the effect of a balanced budget multiplier which is 0.75 in year 1, but falls to zero in year 3 and is −0.6 by year 6.

It is clear that the Treasury model, even as it stands, does have properties consistent with the existence of crowding out. Incorporation of other possible effects would be likely to reinforce these characteristics. This does not prove that the economy works this way, of course, but it does indicate that the question of crowding out must be taken seriously, even by Keynesians.

New Oxford or Old Glasgow: Bacon and Eltis

A particular version of the crowding out thesis that has had a great deal of attention in the UK, through the publication of a series of articles in the *Sunday Times*, is due to Bacon and Eltis (1976). Their basic point would seem to be the same as that made by Adam Smith exactly two centuries earlier, which is that, by the expansion of the public sector, there has been a 'perversion of some portion of the annual produce which had before been destined for the maintenance of productive labour, towards that of unproductive labour.'

Bacon and Eltis pursue their argument by dividing the economy into two sectors. The two sectors are defined by whether or not they produce a 'marketed' output. 'The economy's market sector must produce all exports . . . all investment and all the goods and services that workers buy. It is to be noted that the market sector will include the nationalised industries in so far as these cover their costs through sales of output, as well as the private sectors of modern economies. It will exclude public services which are provided free of charge.' (p. 123)

Bacon and Eltis base their analysis upon an identity. This is:

7.1 $\quad i_m + b_m \equiv e_m - c_u - i_u$

> The proportion of marketed output that can be reinvested in the market sector (i_m) plus the proportion of marketed output

that can be exported net (b_m) is definitionally equal to the rate of surplus of marketed output in the market sector (e_m) less the proportions of marketed output that are used up in consumption (c_u) and investment (i_u) outside the market sector.

Only marketed goods can go into exports, investment and towards satisfying personal consumption expenditure. The 'surplus' of the marketed sector is equal to its total output less what is consumed by the workers in the market sector themselves. This surplus of goods can either be reinvested in the market sector, exported or used up in the non-market sector in the form of consumption and investment. The basic Bacon and Eltis thesis is that Britain's growth and balance of payments problems can be substantially explained by the fact that non-market sector absorption of market sector surplus has crowded out market sector investment and exports.

It is a small step now to identify the non-market sector with the non-industrial public sector, including all those supported by social services such as old age pensioners. In these terms the argument is that expenditure and especially employment in the public sector is too great for the 'health' of the economy. This diagnosis is supported by a casual glance at productivity trends which show that productivity rises in the market sector whereas it is static in the public sector. Diversion of resources into the public sector thus reduces the average productivity growth for the economy as a whole. This is a dangerous argument, however, because public sector output is typically *measured* by its labour input. So there is no way productivity in the public sector can rise – by definition.

The Bacon and Eltis taxonomy undoubtedly provides an interesting framework within which to view the economy. However, their methodology at best establishes correlations but not causation. They do not establish that growth in the marketed sector, *which would otherwise have happened*, was prevented by the employment of resources, especially labour, in the public sector. The upward trend in unemployment over the last two decades would testify to that. Indeed, the argument could just as easily be reversed. Because of the slow output growth in the industrial sector coupled with a continued productivity growth, there has been a decline in the demand for labour in industry. As a result it is essential to expand other forms of employment. This argument has become even stronger in recent years.

One of the statistics used by Bacon and Eltis to support their thesis is the ratio of non-industrial to industrial employment. This ratio rose in the UK from 0.97 in 1961 to 1.3 in 1974, a percentage increase of 34% which was more than double the percentage rise in any comparable country. However, even after this big rise, it is worth noting that this ratio in the UK is still considerably smaller than in the USA and about the same as in Japan and France.

Even more worrying for Bacon and Eltis, however, is the breakdown of the categories of public sector employment. The biggest growth in employment between 1961 and 1974 seems to be in medical services and education. It is hard to believe that nurses and schoolteachers could just as easily have been employed as car workers. However, it is abundantly clear that in most other economies, health services and education are *marketed* products. It is quite possible that, if these services had been sold and priced through the market, employment in them would have grown even faster though the significance of such an expansion would be far from clear.

The important point to notice here is that many of the services provided by the public sector such as health, education, police and leisure services could well be luxury goods. In other words, demand for them would rise more than in proportion to real income growth. There can be no presumption about the 'correct' size of the public sector without some analysis of the underlying demand for the goods involved. Even if these publicly produced goods were to be a constant proportion of total national output, the underlying production functions would lead to a *growing* proportion of all employment being in the public sector. Public sector services, being labour intensive, require a bigger growth of labour input for any given growth of output than do manufacturing industries. It now seems absurd to suggest that the growth of manufacturing industry has been constrained by excessive public sector employment.

While it would not be surprising to find a growth of government consumption more than in proportion to the growth in national income, particularly when health services and education are provided by the state, it is not at all clear that this has happened to any significant degree in the UK. Chrystal and Alt (1979), for example, find that the elasticity of government consumption with respect to GDP is not significantly different from unity over the period 1955–74. They also find that British experience is not at all out of line with other countries:

Britain was a relatively big spender in 1955, with 17 per cent of GDP going to government consumption; in 1974, the figure was 20.5 per cent, smaller than in Denmark, Sweden and the US and similar to that of Germany. Moreover, the growth of the government share in GDP was comparatively slow in Britain over these two decades, outstripping only the expenditure growth in Italy, the Netherlands, France and the US . . . these modest results do suggest that the British experience is not unique and that there are clearly no grounds for assuming that government expenditure in Britain has grown atypically fast, or takes an atypically large share of national income.

A more detailed analysis of the causes of government growth as well as evidence from Britain and a number of other countries is available in Alt and Chrystal (1983, chapters 8-10). Their general conclusion is that what has to be explained is not the excessive growth or variability of government but, rather, its remarkable stability in relation to national income both in Britain and in many other countries. Government behaviour is characterised by 'inertia' more than it is by any other simple hypothesis.

Summary

The conclusion reached in this chapter is that, while crowding out must realistically be accepted as a property of reasonable macroeconomic models, it is far from an established truth that overexpansion of government expenditure has *actually* been responsible for any significant crowding out of the private sector in the UK in the last 25 years. Controversy in this area will, no doubt, continue indefinitely.

Notes

1 Apart from any influence *Capitalism and Freedom* may have had.
2 What the St. Louis result really amounts to is that prices are proportional to the money stock and real government expenditure is a stable proportion of real GDP.

8
Business Cycles: Causes and Control

Many leading economists who worked in the first half of the twentieth century regarded the explanation of the recurrent cycles in the economy as a high priority. Interest in this area died down somewhat in the 1950s and 1960s both because cycles had ceased to be a major problem and because the theoretical focus of Keynesian economics was on the determination of the level of income at a specific point in time. Such dynamic theory as there was was more concerned with the characteristics of stable growth paths than with cycles about such paths. This is not to say that there was no concern with cycles, merely that the dominant view was that the new Keynesian policy tools ensured that cycles need no longer be a problem. This view was reinforced by the self-evident absence of major cycles which was interpreted by many to mean that these policy tools were highly effective. There is, of course, another interpretation of these events, as we shall see.

An understanding of the nature and causes of business cycles is at the heart of policy controversy between Keynesians and Monetarists. A different explanation is offered by New Classical economists, notably Robert Lucas, which, as we have already seen, is even more damaging to the case for active stabilisation policy than the Monetarist arguments. At the centre of the problem is the question of whether the private sector of the economy is basically stable and whether government intervention makes it more stable or less stable. This distinction was emphasised by Modigliani (1977) in his presidential address to the American Economic Association:

> In reality, the distinguishing feature of the Monetarist school and the real issue of disagreement with non-Monetarists is not Monetarism, but

rather the role that should probably be assigned to stabilisation policies. Non-Monetarists accept what I regard to be the fundamental practical message of the General Theory: that a private enterprise economy using an intangible money needs to be stabilised, can be stabilised and therefore should be stabilised by appropriate monetary and fiscal policies. Monetarists, by contrast, take the view that there is no serious need to stabilise the economy; that even if there were a need, it could not be done, for stabilisation policies would be more likely to increase than to decrease instability, and, at least some Monetarists would, I believe, go so far as to hold that, even in the unlikely event that stabilisation policies could on balance prove beneficial, the government should not be trusted with the necessary power. (p. 1.)

These issues are now of urgent importance. Most countries have been through two major depressions in the last ten years (1974–5 and 1981–3, though the precise timing differs from country to country) more serious than any since the 1930s. As a result of this, it should be no surprise that there has been a revival of interest in business cycle theory.

Theory of Business Cycles

One of the most famous students of the business cycle, Joseph Schumpeter (1939), identified three different amplitudes of cycle in the previous 150 years. These he named after writers who had noticed them previously. There was a 60 year wave (Kondratieff), a 10 year cycle (Juglar) and a 40 month cycle (Kitchin). It is the shortest of these which is the one most economists refer to as the business cycle or trade cycle. Subsequent empirical research, particularly that in the US associated with the National Bureau of Economic Research (NBER), has concluded that business cycles cannot be accurately characterised by periodicity. The time profile is, in fact, irregular. What does characterise these cycles, however, is a remarkably common pattern of co-movements of aggregate economic series.

> The principal among these are the following:
> (i) Output movements across broadly defined sectors move together. (In Mitchell's (Wesley C. Mitchell 1941) terminology they exhibit high conformity, in modern time series language, they have high coherence.)
> (ii) Production of producer and consumer durables exhibits much greater amplitude than does the production of non-durables.

(iii) Production and prices of agricultural goods and natural resources have lower than average conformity.
(iv) Business profits show high conformity and much greater amplitude than other series.
(v) Prices generally are procyclical.
(vi) Short-term interest rates are procyclical, long-term rates slightly so.
(vii) Monetary aggregates and velocity measures are procyclical. (Lucas 1977, p. 9.)

Keynesian Approach

While the literature contains large numbers of attempts to explain cycles (see, for example, R. A. Gordon 1961, Chs. 12 and 13), attention here is restricted to the main differences between the Macro contenders.

Keynesian economics would appear to have no serious difficulty in accounting for these stylised facts. The initial event would be a change in exogenous expenditures such as exports or investment. This would be transmitted through the economy by a combination of the multiplier effect and the accelerator (Samuelson 1939). The latter reflects the induced effect on investment of the change in output. Upswings or downswings may be explosive but constrained by ceilings (resource constraints) and floors (net investment cannot be negative) as, for example, in Hicks (1950). Alternatively, the dynamics of the economy may, themselves, be cyclical (Matthews 1959) – possibly damped cycles, possibly explosive. To illustrate this let us consider a specific case set out by Matthews (*op. cit.* p. 23).

The accelerator derives from the fact that a given capital stock is required to produce a constant level of output. This means net investment (increases in capital – depreciation is ignored) must be associated with *growing* output. Assume that there is a lag between changes in output and investment, so

8.1 $\quad I_t = v(Y_{t-1} - Y_{t-2})$

The consumption function is the familiar one

8.2 $\quad C_t = \alpha + \beta Y_t$

The solution for current income when 8.1 and 8.2 are substituted into $Y = C + I$ is

8.3 $$Y_t = \frac{v}{1-\beta}(Y_{t-1} - Y_{t-2}) + \frac{\alpha}{1-\beta}$$

This is a second order difference equation, the course of which will depend on the precise values of the parameter (v and β in this case), but it is quite likely[1] that a once-and-for-all change in exogenous expenditures (α) will lead to *cycles* in Y. Consider Matthews' numerical example which is set out in table 8.1. Take the values of v and β as 3/5 and 1/2 respectively. Set the initial values of variables as follows: Income (Y) = 100, Capital (K) = 60, Investment (I) = 0, Autonomous Consumption (α) = 50. Then, in the third period, α increases to 75 and stays at the new higher level. The immediate impact is a multiplier effect on income of 50 ($1/(1-\beta) = 2$).

Table 8.1

Period	α	I	Y	C	K (beginning of period)
1	50	0	100	100	60
2	50	0	100	100	60
3	75	0	150	150	60
4	75	30	210	180	60
5	75	36	222	186	90
6	75	7	164	157	126
7	75	−35	81	115	133
8	75	−50	50	100	99
9	75	−19	113	131	49
10	75	38	225	188	30
11	75	68	285	218	68
12	75	36	222	186	135

In the next period investment starts to rise because income rose the period before. The investment has a further upward multiplier effect on income, so next period investment is a bit higher, though only a little. So the rate of increase in income slows down and this leads to a reduction of investment which, itself, leads to a downturn of income etc.

The central elements of this mechanism still seem highly plausible. The model is, of course, highly simplified and would in reality have to include many other structural constraints. Nonetheless, in an IS-LM type framework augmented by a simple Phillips

Curve, this model could account for all the stylised facts set out above. Seen as caused by a shifting IS curve, the cycle would evidence positive correlations between output and all of prices, profits, interest rates and velocity. The accelerator is also a very convincing reason why cycles in capital goods industries are of much greater amplitude than in consumer goods industries. However, the analysis also carries the strong implication that government behaviour could change all this. In the above example, if government expenditure had been included in the analysis, a reduction of G by 25 in period three would have left income stable. Similarly, a government reaction function of the form $G = -v(Y_{t-1} - Y_{t-2})$ would eliminate the cycle by offsetting the accelerator.

Monetarist Approach

The Monetarist approach to the business cycle is rather different from this and is most clearly evident in the work of Milton Friedman and Anna Schwartz (1963 a and b). It cannot be claimed that monetary factors were ignored in Keynesian-style explanations – they were not (See Hicks 1950, Ch. 11; Harrod 1936, Ch. 3; Matthews 1959, Ch. 8). Indeed, the trade cycle had been described by one of Keynes' contemporaries, R. G. Hawtrey, as 'a purely monetary phenomenon' (though Hawtrey could hardly be described as a Keynesian). What was different about the work of Friedman and Schwartz (apart from the detailed empirical evidence they produced to support their case) was the emphatic insistence on the importance of the money stock, rather than on credit conditions and interest rates in general. Most stories would have tightening credit as associated with the slow down, and easy credit associated with the upturn. Friedman and Schwartz argued that changes in money were the dominant cause of cycles and that these changes were predominantly exogenous. The following statements are the main findings of Friedman and Schwartz (1963a):

> There is unquestionably a close relation between the variability of the stock of money and the variability of income. This relation has persisted over some nine decades and appears no different at the end of the period than at the beginning . . . (p. 43)
> There is a one-to-one relation between monetary changes and changes

in money income and prices. Changes in money income and prices have, in every case, been accompanied by a chance in the rate of growth of the money stock, in the same direction and of appreciable magnitude, and there are no comparable disturbances in the rate of growth of the money stock unaccompanied by changes in money income and prices.

The changes in the stock of money cannot consistently be explained by the contemporary changes in money income and prices. The changes in the stock of money can generally be attributed to specific historical circumstances that are not in turn attributable to contemporary changes in money income and prices. Hence, if the consistent relation between money and income is not pure coincidence, *it must reflect an influence running from money to business*. (p. 50)

. . . Our survey of experience leads us to conjecture that longer-period changes in money income produced by a changed secular rate of growth of the money stock are reflected mainly in different price behaviour rather than in different rates of growth of output; whereas the shorter-period changes in the rate of growth of the money stock are capable of exerting a sizable influence on the rate of growth of output as well. (p. 53)

Even if the above statements are accepted, we still do not have a reason to believe that a step change in the rate of growth of the money stock will generate anything but an (ultimate) step change in the rate of inflation and a one-off temporary effect on the level of real output. How does this provide the basis for a theory of business cycles? The answer provided by Friedman and Schwartz is that the transmission mechanism contains forces that will produce overshooting. The principal of these is associated with the fact that the demand for real money balances depends upon the rate of inflation (this is the opportunity cost of holding money relative to goods). Suppose there is a step increase in the rate of growth of money. In equilibrium there will be a similar step increase in the rate of inflation. However, as a result of the higher inflation, demand for real money balances will fall. This means that the price *level* must be higher relative to the *nominal* money stock than it was initially. Therefore, during the transition to the new equilibrium, the rate of inflation must overshoot its steady state value. This temporary overshooting of inflation will lead people to run down their real money balances too far. As they build them up again the inflation rate must be below its equilibrium level etc. The run down of money balances phase will, of course, be associated with upturns in business activity and *vice versa* for the build-up of money balances.

In purely mechanical terms there are obvious similarities between this explanation of cycles and the accelerator mechanism. In one case the dynamics result from the fact that the stock demand for one variable (money) depends upon the rate of change of another (prices). In the other case a flow demand (investment – itself, the change in the stock of capital) depends on the rate of change of another variable (income). In both cases the time paths of endogenous variables may be described by difference or differential equations which, depending upon the parameters of the system, may generate cycles once disturbed. In terms of their implication for policy, however, the Keynesian and Monetarist explanations are very different.

The main policy difference derives from differences as to the source of disturbances. For Keynesians the shocks come from changes in autonomous expenditures, such as exports, or shifts in private expenditures, such as investment. This reflects intrinsic instabilities of the market economy and it is the job of government to try to spot these movements and offset them by changes in its own behaviour. For Monetarists the shocks are primarily changes in the rate of growth of money and, at least in the modern world, control of the money stock is the responsibility of central monetary authorities. The shocks, therefore, are primarily due to control failures on the part of government or governmental agencies. Hence, the conclusion that the discretionary powers of these authorities should be reduced and they should be made to adhere to a more or less rigid growth rule for the money stock.

Even if shocks are identified as being from other sources, monetary policy should not be used as a tool of stabilisation policy because it is too clumsy. In Friedman's well worn phrase, the impact of monetary policy is subject to 'long and variable lags'. As a result, a policy which is intended to be stabilising may, in reality, be destabilising. A stimulus, for example, intended to help the economy out of a depression may add fuel to a subsequent boom because its effects are felt with a lag. The variability of such lags makes the stabilisation role of monetary policy severely limited.

New Classical Approach

The New Classical approach to business cycles contains elements of both the accelerator mechanism (as, indeed, could the Monetarist story, though it is not emphasised) and monetary shocks. However, in one respect the New Classical economists have made a major break with the post World War Two macroeconomic tradition. This is their insistence on developing an *equilibrium theory* of the business cycle. The reason for this insistence is the problem posed by the Lucas Critique (discussed in Chapter 4) rather than the inability of earlier theories to explain the general pattern of past cycles.

> . . . The ability of a model to imitate actual behaviour . . . has almost nothing to do with its ability to make accurate *conditional* forecasts, to answer questions of the form: how *would* behaviour have differed had certain policies been different in specified ways? . . . Any disequilibrium model, constructed by simply codifying the decision rules which agents have found it useful to use over some previous sample period, without explaining why these rules were used, will be of no use in predicting the consequences of non trivial policy changes. (Lucas 1977, p. 12)
>
> Before the 1930s economists did not recognise a need for a special branch of economics, with its own special postulates, designed to explain the business cycle. Keynes founded that sub-discipline, called 'macroeconomics', because he thought explaining the characteristics of business cycles was impossible within the discipline imposed by classical economic theory, a discipline imposed by its insistence on adherence to the two postulates (a) that markets clear and (b) that agents act in their own self-interest. The outstanding facts that seemed impossible to reconcile with these two postulates were the length and severity of business depressions and the large-scale unemployment they entailed . . .
>
> . . . The research line being pursued by some of us involves the attempt to discover a particular econometrically testable equilibrium theory of the business cycle, one that can serve as the foundation for quantitative analysis of macroeconomic policy. There is no denying that this approach is counter-revolutionary, for it presupposes that Keynes and his followers were wrong to give up on the possibility that an equilibrium theory could account for the business cycle. (Lucas and Sargent 1981b, pp. 304–306).

It should be immediately obvious that to have an *equilibrium* theory of cycles requires a different concept of equilibrium from that normally used in textbook economics. Equilibrium is not, in this sense, a state of rest. Rather, it means that at each point of time actors respond optimally to the prices they perceive (which are being perpetually disturbed) and that markets should clear, given the supply and demand responses by actors to their perceptions of prices. In other words, the economy will be describable by a stable statistical process rather than by displaying constant values of all variables. The idea of optimising individuals should not be alien to economists. However, the statement that markets perpetually clear at first sight seems outrageous. We shall see that it is not so outrageous and amounts to little more than an analytical device. It should not be interpreted as a statement about the real world, though unfortunately it often is. For example, it does not deny the existence of registered unemployed.

The central mechanism that generates the cycle is the 'surprise' supply relationship that was described in Chapter 4 above. When applied to the explanation of business cycles (Lucas 1975, 1977), the story contains elements of both speculative supply behaviour (Lucas and Rapping 1969) and signal extraction (Lucas 1972, 1973). Consider an individual self-employed producer. He has to decide each period how much to work and therefore produce, and he also has to decide how much to invest (that is, increase his capital stock). Both these decisions are made on the basis of one piece of current information – the price of his output. He learns about everything else going on in the economy with a lag except that, as before, he does know the probability distribution of real and nominal shocks.

Let us suppose that our actor observes a rise in the current price of his output. How should he react? As before, it depends on the extent to which he thinks this is a shift of (real) relative prices in his favour as opposed to a rise in the general price level. To the extent that he perceives it as real, he also has to decide whether it is temporary or permanent. If it is temporary, he should work harder now and take his leisure later when the return to effort will be lower. If it is permanent, it will pay to increase his capacity by investing. The claim is that since he has to make all these decisions on the basis of a single price signal, the optimal response will be a weighted average. The weights depend on the relative variances of real and nominal shocks as before. The price rise will be associated with both a higher current output and higher level of investment. This relation between output and investment can be thought of as an accelerator, though it will be damped as compared to the Keynesian accelerator. Investment will only respond to output changes perceived to be permanent.

Two important problems remain. Why do random shocks generate cycles of considerable duration? Why are the cycles evident in the aggregate rather than simply averaging out across the economy? For the New Classical business cyclist persistence is a serious problem but not insuperable. There is no necessary inconsistency between the randomness of shocks and the fact that output and employment changes are auto-correlated. Two factors in combination are used by Lucas (1975) to explain the duration of cycles. One is the lag in receipt of information; the other is the durability of capital goods. The role of lagged information has been discussed above. Obviously, the longer the information lag the longer will be the full-adjustment period. This would not matter so much if decisions were costlessly reversable. However, once changes are made in the capital stock this is no longer true because capital formation is assumed to be irreversible. Mistakes made in one period will continue to affect output in future periods – hence, the persistence of effect resulting from a random shock.

Why, then, is there a tendency for all sectors to expand and contract together? The answer is that the nature of the shock cannot be a random shift between markets or, indeed, any kind of disturbance that will wash out in the aggregate. Nor can it be an aggregate supply shock because this would lead to a negative correlation between price and output which is not the typical pattern of business cycles. The strongest candidate is an aggregate monetary disturbance, since this is the most likely to affect the price signals in all markets simultaneously. It should go without saying that this monetary disturbance has to be unanticipated.

However, even a fully anticipated change in the rate of monetary expansion will have real effects if prices are not perfectly flexible for the same reasons as there is overshooting in the Monetarist business cycle. If there is a step increase in the rate of monetary growth this will lead to a corresponding step increase in the inflation rate. Demand for real money balances will fall. This can only be achieved at a higher relative price level. If the increased growth rate of money is *fully anticipated*, the price level will jump up at the initial point in time. Similarly, an anticipated lowering of the rate of monetary growth will both lower the inflation rate and cause an immediate downward jump in the price level. Friedman and Schwartz implicitly assume that prices are sticky so that some of the adjustment pressure is felt on output. It is hard to believe that prices are so flexible that there would not be real effects in any realistic economy. However flexible prices are, it is hard to believe that the price level could jump downwards overnight in immediate response to the announcement of a tighter monetary policy. This, of course, reinforces the case for monetary causes of business cycles, but it would not meet with the approval of New Classical economists because of the arbitrary presumption in favour of price stickiness. However, the assumption of a jump in prices is also problematic because at the point in time at which the jump takes place the return to nominal assets is either plus infinity or minus infinity. If this jump is anticipated, the model will be explosive. New Classical economists handle this problem by assuming it away. The economy is simply assumed to jump to the new stable (saddle) path. How a real world economy could jump in this way is not a question that seems to cause concern!

It is this assumption that prices adjust continuously to clear markets that has been the cause of the most serious misgivings about New Classical economics among economists. While markets do exist in which prices are determined to clear the market at the time (such as commodity markets and foreign exchange markets), most goods and services are traded in what Hicks (1974) calls 'fix-price markets' and Okun (1981) calls 'customer markets'. Certainly the rhetoric of New Classical economics is inconsistent with arbitrary stickiness in prices. However, in reality the disagreement is more apparent than real. It is an issue of semantics rather than economics. This is because, as we have just seen, New Classical economists have to introduce *imperfections and rigidities of some kind* in order to explain real world data. The effect of this is to introduce auto-correlation into activity series (such as GDP) so that the series becomes describable by a difference or differential equation as above. Once in this form, the theory is *observationally equivalent* (Sargent 1976) to a large number of other theories including versions of the ones outlined above. There may be no way of discriminating between them from the data alone.

In behavioural terms this has an obvious interpretation. The price stickiness view of markets has some actors at the *market place* frustrated because they cannot buy or sell at the going price. This price does not adjust immediately to reflect this excess demand or supply. We would commonly say that the market does not clear. In the New Classical set up the price does clear the market made up of the actors who actually express the demands or supplies actively at a point in time *at the market place*, but it does not reflect the demands and supplies of actors who are delayed in their response because of poor information or being locked into the wrong location or equipment because of past mistakes. In the first view, for example, the unemployed worker is knocking at the factory gate, yet the employer does not reduce wages immediately to make it profitable to employ him. In the second view, there are no workers left outside the factory gate today. All who turned up today struck a wage bargain with the employer such that all get employed today. However, there are other workers who would work at that wage agreed today. It is just that they will not get there until after they hear about it and then have time to move house and arrange transport etc. Either way, there is slow adjustment and it is surely a matter of taste which way the problem is specified. The former conforms to many of our (perhaps Keynesian) prejudices, whereas the latter may well offer methodological advantages. These are that the reasons for the slow adjustment have to be explicitly stated and, as a result, can be formally modelled. It does, however, seem unnecessarily narrow to rule out, *a priori*, some form of price stickiness which can be justified by optimising models such as that discussed in the implicit contracts literature.

The implications of the New Classical approach are, of course, even more cautionary for stabilisation policy than was the Monetarist approach. Here, though, the strictures are much stronger. It is not the problem of long and varied lags. Rather, it is the fact that *any* systematic policy will come to be anticipated by actors. This argument is set out in detail in Chapter 4. Stabilisation policy would be beneficial if the authorities had superior information or were able to react quicker than private actors.

How, then, do these broad approaches to business cycles stand up to the evidence? This is not the place to discuss the evidence in detail, but it is worth considering how we should explain the obvious contrast of experience between the 1950s and 1960s on the one hand, and the inter-war and post-1970 periods on the other. Keynesians would presumably argue that the 1950s and 1960s were the example, *par excellence*, of what can be achieved by the successful application of Keynesian principles. Against this, a strong case can be made for the contrary point of view on the grounds that the 1950s and 1960s were, above all, a period of *monetary stability*. The US was following (until the mid-1960s) conservative policies and the rest of the world pegged their currencies to the dollar. It was the attempt by the US to follow Keynesian expansionist policies that caused the system to break down. Subsequent events are to be explained by big swings in monetary policy (accompanied by exchange rate instability) which have been responsible for the two depressions of the last decade. At least in the UK case, it is hard to believe that the poor performance of the UK economy in the 1970s has not had something to do with monetary shocks – notably the excessive stimulus of 1971–3 and the excessive tightening of 1973–74 and 1979–81. The mechanism for the transmission of these effects is discussed in Chapter 5.

Political Business Cycles

A further alleged cause of economic cycles arises from the fact that economic policy is made by elected politicians in the context of political institutions. Such policy may reflect the political objectives of the government. For example, to the extent that popularity is influenced by the state of the economy a government may hope to improve its re-election chances by generating boom conditions just before a general election. A slump would presumably follow after the election. Such a pattern, where booms coincide with elections, is known as a political business cycle. One American author (Tufte 1978) has gone so far as to argue that the cycles in the US economy are, more or less, all election-related. His evidence, however, is unconvincing except for the case of the 1972 Presidential election. Then, there was a substantial rise in Federal transfer payments (Veterans' benefits etc) just a week before the election.

The most explicit theoretical case for a political business cycle relies upon the government 'riding' the short-term Phillips curve. This argument is explicitly set out in Nordhaus (1975) and provides the basis of his claim that 'democracy causes inflation'. Consider figure 8.1.

The curves labelled P are short-run Phillips curves, higher numbers reflecting higher levels of expected inflation. The curves labelled U are social indifference curves, the points along which will generate the same vote for the government – lower numbers reflect higher utility and a higher vote. The curve LRP is the long-run Phillips curve (Nordhaus takes it to be non-vertical, though this is not important so long as it is steeper than the P curves).

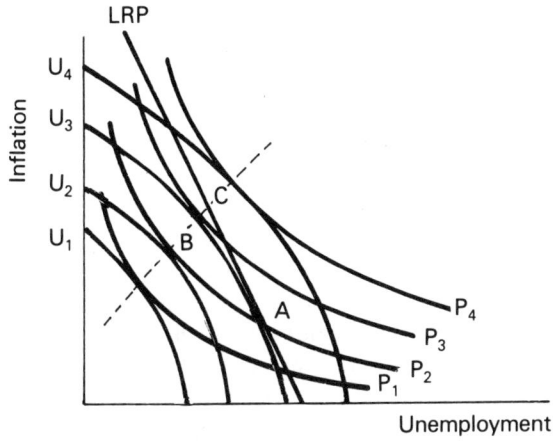

Figure 8.1

Each government finds itself on a particular P curve such as P_2. The vote-maximising strategy will be to run the economy at point B which yields the highest possible vote. During the next period, however, since B is to the left of the long-run Phillips curve, the economy will be on a higher P curve like P_3. This process will converge to a point like C which is on the *LRP* curve and, therefore, stable. This is sub-optimal because point A is the point of highest sustainable social welfare. The political process has generated higher inflation and lower unemployment than would be preferred.

It is easy to tell a story about cycles in this framework. Governments simply ride up the P curve to the highest U curve at election time. Then, after the election, they depress the economy – to the right of *LRP* – so that they find the economy on the lowest possible P curve by the time of the next election. They then generate a boom again in time to be re-elected.

Plausible as this account may be, the evidence for it is remarkably weak. Even the proponents of this kind of 'political' view of policy (Frey 1978) seem to have given up looking for electoral cycles in the *targets* of economic policy such as inflation and unemployment. Also, the evidence concerning the influence of the state of the economy on political popularity and voting is not at all clear cut. It is certainly true that popularity can be significantly related to economic variables for some historical time period. The problem is that the results are heavily sample-dependent. For almost any other time period they will be substantially different. Particularly strong swings in coefficients are discovered when the results for the 1960s are extended into the 1970s.

An alternative way of looking at the question is to ask whether the electorate can be fooled in the short run, and whether the government acts as if they can. Asking the question this way focuses attention on the electorate's expectations, as well as upon the current state of affairs. If electors are fully 'rational' they will anticipate the post-election deflation and so there will be no benefit for the incumbent party in running a pre-election boom. Macrae (1977) incorporates expectations explicitly by distinguishing between a myopic and a strategic electorate. A myopic electorate only considers the current state of the economy, whereas strategic voters have a longer time horizon. Macrae's results for the US appear to show that the government assumed myopia from 1960–8 but strategic voting before and after. Applying Macrae's model to the UK, Chrystal and Alt (1981) conclude that 'the myopic hypothesis never significantly out-performs the strategic hypothesis'. And they are thus led to conclude that '. . . while on some occasions the government may indeed have manipulated unemployment with a vote loss or social welfare function in mind, there is no evidence that the desire to win the next election, as distinct from remaining in office as long as possible, was the motivation'. Thus, we must conclude that the evidence for a political business cycle in Britain is negative. There can be no presumption that the government manipulates the economy on the assumption of a short-sighted electorate.

What appears to be a more sophisticated attempt to incorporate political goals into economic policy analysis is provided by Frey and Schneider (1978). They develop what they call a 'politico-economic' model of the UK. There are two elements to this. First, government popularity depends upon certain economic variables. Second, various components of government expenditure are shown to be altered as a result of popularity, the time before elections and the political make-up of the incumbent party. Chrystal and Alt (1981) show that if government expenditure and revenue are related to trend GDP, virtually all the political factors drop out. The only significant political factor to remain is that transfers are higher under Labour than Conservative Governments, as might be expected. We must, therefore, conclude that electoral-cyclical and politico-economic explanations of budgetary policy in the UK are not well founded. A fuller discussion of these issues is available in Alt and Chrystal (1983).

Summary

Business cycles and their study have staged a revival. Keynesian business cycles relied on multiplier and accelerator interaction in response to exogenous expenditure changes. Monetarists emphasised changes in monetary growth as the source of cycles. The New Classical analysis also relies on exogenous monetary disturbances, but has the novel feature of an equilibrium methodology. While these approaches may generate models which are observationally equivalent, they have very different implications for the role of government. In the Keynesian view governments could and should attempt to stabilise the economy. For the others, governments are the major source of disturbances. Their discretion should therefore be limited.

Note

1 In this case the model is explosive if $v/(1-\beta)$ is greater than one and cycles if it is less than four.

9
Supply Shocks

Macroeconomics was developed as a framework for analysing the transmission of aggregate demand changes through the economy. This framework has proved inadequate for handling disturbances which originate on the supply side. Traditional macroeconomic models have a production sector which has a single homogenous output made for the most part with a single variable input. This framework is inadequate for the analysis of changes such as a major price rise in one of several variable inputs or the emergence of a major new extractive industry.

The oil price rise of 1973 and the expansion of North Sea oil production have been too important to be ignored. Chapter 6, for example, gave evidence that the dramatic decline in manufacturing employment in the UK since 1979 may not be unrelated to North Sea oil production. It is beyond the scope of this book to present a formal structural analysis of the UK economy. However, it is important to realise that such an analysis is necessary if the policy implications of these changes are to be fully understood. Aggregate demand policies have a place, but this may not be it.

The 1973 Oil Price Rise

It is instructive to recall the way in which the 1973 oil price rise was analysed by various commentators on the UK economy. The analysis of this Section draws on Miller (1976). Remember that the problem at that time was the quadrupling of the oil price. Virtually all oil was imported.

The principal way in which the policy makers in the UK looked at the problem seems to be through orthodox Keynesian eyes. In the context of Model I, imports are a leakage from the circular flow system so they affect the economy just like a massive increase in indirect taxes. The tax revenue, however, accrues to foreigners. A typical figure quoted for the size of this increased import bill was £1500m. A clear example of how a Keynesian should see this problem is provided by G.D.N. Worswick, the Director of the National Institute, in his evidence to the Public Expenditure Committee (1974):

> If nothing is done about the substantial rise in the price of oil, that figure of £1500m will be taken out of the system. There will be that much less spent in the following period and there will be a contraction of demand and a contraction of output in due course together with a contraction of employment. In this case the rise in the price of oil has a profound contractionary effect on all countries. (p. 42)
>
> ... When the government is making up its balance of the budget over the year as a whole it must allow for the fact that real consumption will be less than it would be if the price of oil had not risen ... The present Chancellor has said that he wishes to have a new look at the situation later in the year. As I see it now, he would need to be expansionary. (p. 43)

The effect of a rise in the value of imports can easily be analysed in the context of Model I. The initial position in figure 9.1 is with the aggregate expenditure line $C+I+G+X-P_0$. This gives an initial level of income equal to Y_0. An increase in the value of imports represents a greater 'leakage' of expenditure from the circular flow, so the aggregate expenditure line falls to $C+I+G+X-P_1$. This will lead, through the downward multiplier effect, to a lower level of income Y_1. We would normally expect this downward fall in income to be accompanied by an increase in unemployment. This is why the Keynesian response to the oil crisis was to point to the dangers of a depression and to propose a reflation. Offsetting policies on the part of the government would simply involve either increasing expenditure or reducing taxes so that aggregate expenditure shifts back towards its original position. The balance of payments deficit is thus reinforced.

The problem, of course, is not really as simple as that. For one thing we have said nothing at all about inflation. More importantly in the present context, however, the concept of income is ambiguous. The simplest way to see this is to ask what would have

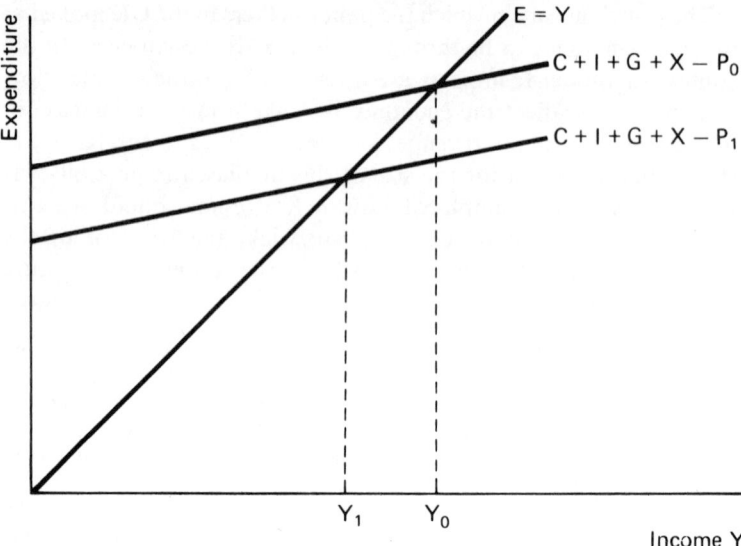

Figure 9.1

happened if the elasticity of demand for oil had been unity. The import bill would have remained constant following the oil price rise. But does this mean that domestic income would have been unchanged? The answer is clearly no. Although there is no direct change in real GDP because physical output and the GDP deflator are unchanged, since the value of the things we produce has fallen relative to the things we buy from abroad, domestic income has unambiguously fallen in a real and more general way. What this means is that, even if there was no impact effect on unemployment, the possibilities for domestic absorption have fallen. There has to be a fall in domestic real income.

While domestic income has to fall owing to this terms-of-trade loss, it does not necessarily follow that some reflation should not be applied. Miller argues that the view at the time was that the required fall in income was less than the fall from Y_0 to Y_1 in figure 9.1 and this is why expansionary measures were advocated. The problem with this approach, of course, is that even if it were successful in avoiding unemployment in the short run, it certainly increases inflation, which many would argue would increase unemployment even more in the long run. The outcome would appear to be consistent with this latter view. Unemployment did not rise as rapidly in the UK through 1974 and 1975 as it did in many other countries, whereas the inflationary experience was considerably worse in the UK. Unemployment in the UK, however, continued to rise subsequently, though in many countries it started to fall after 1976.

Miller concludes that while Keynesians were not unaware that there would be 'imported inflation', they believed that a gradual return to full employment should be possible through 'expansionary fiscal policy and permissive monetary policy'. In strict contrast to this Miller believes that '. . . the Monetarist logic predicted no inflation or recession as a consequence of the change in the terms of trade so long as fiscal and monetary policy were unchanged'. Miller bases his analysis of the Monetarist position upon the summary of the evidence presented by Laidler to the Expenditure Committee. However, this summary was either written by the Committee members themselves or by the Civil Service. Laidler's own evidence does not bear the interpretation Miller puts upon it (nor, in reality, does the summary).

The first point to notice about Laidler's evidence is that he is absolutely clear that '. . . If oil prices have gone up and the terms of trade have moved against this country, we are poorer, and it is impossible for people to protect their standards of living against that'. Secondly, he answers the question about the price level by reference to an earlier point about the net effect of a decrease in indirect taxes financed by higher direct taxes, at a given level of national income. There he says, 'If there were no net decrease in purchasing power, I cannot see how *ultimately* the price level would be different'. In contrast, the Director of the National Institute was reported to have argued, by analogy to an increase in indirect taxes, that inflation would rise because people would ask for and obtain higher wages to compensate for the higher oil price. Indirect taxes rising would be inflationary and more inflationary than income taxes of equal yield. To this Laidler replied: '. . . If it is the case that people notice that indirect taxes have changed the purchasing power of their gross incomes before they notice that direct ones have done so, I cannot believe that this is any more than a very *short-run* phenomenon. It is one thing, in any case, to ask for a wage increase and another thing to have it granted.'

The overwhelming impression that emerges from Laidler's

evidence, in its entirety, can be expressed as two main points. First, the impact effects of the oil price rise should be clearly distinguished from the ultimate or long-run effects. Second, a clear distinction must be drawn between relative price changes and sustained inflation of the general price level. The oil price rise is a relative price change and, although it will undoubtedly raise the price index in the short run, it will only lead to a *long-run* rise in the price level if it is followed by monetary expansion. An appropriate framework for expounding the Monetarist analysis might be Model III.

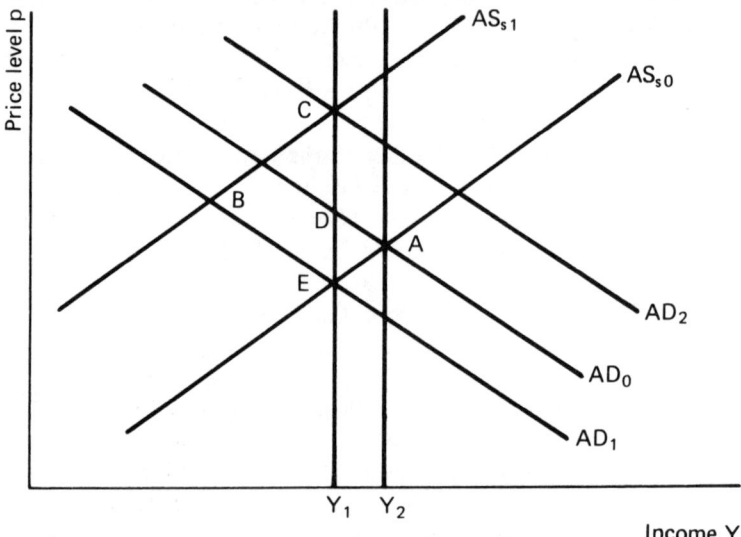

Figure 9.2

Consider the initial position at A in figure 9.2. The short-run aggregate supply curve can be thought of as depending on the expected price level. What then is the effect of a rise in the price of imports? First notice that, although the *physical* production possibilities of the economy are unchanged, since the relative price of domestic output has fallen, we should regard long-run aggregate supply as having fallen from Y_0 to Y_1. This is the terms-of-trade loss. There are two other effects. Firstly, there is a leftward shift of the short-run aggregate supply curve from AS_{S0} to AS_{S1}. This is due to the direct effect of import prices on the domestic price level plus any immediate effect on price expectations. The second effect is the Keynesian one. Aggregate *domestic* demand will move from AD_0 to AD_1 due to the rise in the import bill. Both Monetarists and Keynesians should accept the story so far. The impact effect is a move from A to a position like B. There has been a rise in the price level and an increase in unemployment associated with a decline in domestic output. The disagreement is about the next step in the argument.

The Keynesians do not have a next step. The economy has settled into a depression at B so expansionary fiscal policies are required. Raising aggregate demand will move the economy to C, thereby eliminating unemployment. The problem with this analysis, however, is that even C is not a full equilibrium. This is because AS_{S1} was drawn for an *expected* price level somewhere between that at A and that at B. As these price level expectations are revised upwards, the short-run AS curve will shift up further. If policy makers raise aggregate demand still further to avoid unemployment, this upward spiral will continue, as they found to their cost.

The Monetarist analysis points to the fact that B is not a point of full equilibrium. If the monetary and fiscal pressures which are due to the authorities remain unchanged, the economy will eventually return to a point somewhere in the region of D. This is because excess supply in some markets will cause some prices to fall, so eventually short-run AS will shift back down. Also there will be some northeastward shift of AD due to a change in the pattern of expenditures following the increase in import prices. The ultimate effect of the oil price rise on the import bill will, *ceteris paribus*, be less in the long run than in the short run because expenditure patterns take time to adjust. At D the price level may be slightly higher or lower than at A, but it will not be substantially different.

The problem with this Monetarist analysis is that we have no information as to how long it will be before the economy returns from B to D. The problem with the Keynesian policy prescription is that it necessarily leads to a higher price level and, therefore, to faster inflation in the interim. The key difference in analysis of the problem is that Monetarists see the economy as self-stabilising within a reasonable time period. Keynesians recommended policies to counter the impact effects on the assumption that the economy would not be self-stabilising with any rapidity and the unemployment target should be given high priority.

North Sea Oil

If the oil price rise caused so much trouble when we were an importer, the emergence of a self-sufficiency in oil production should have been of unambiguous benefit. For example, consider the economy to have been initially at D in figure 9.2, on AD_0 and with long-run supply at Y_1. A once-and-for-all increase in oil supply might be considered to shift aggregate supply to Y_2. The economy would then go to A with higher output and lower prices. How, then, could North Sea oil production be associated with rising unemployment as was argued in Chapter 6?

The answer is that the above analysis is not correct. What we have just analysed is something like an autonomous productivity rise in the single homogenous sector that constitutes our macroeconomy. What we need to analyse is change in production in one sector only. The effects are complex because they involve intersectoral resource shifts, intersectoral demand shifts, and changes in the composition of foreign trade and capital flows as well as the aggregate expenditure and output effects which are the traditional domain of macroeconomics. Such structural changes have more commonly been treated within the domain of international trade theory.

A comprehensive analysis from a trade theoretical perspective is available in Corden and Neary (1982). Their model contains two traded goods – oil and manufactures – and one non-traded good – services. What happens, they ask, when there is a production boom in one of the traded goods (oil)? A central conclusion of their analysis is as follows:

> In the simplest of the models considered, which assumed that only labour was mobile between sectors, de-industrialisation (a decline in the non-booming part of the traded goods sector, assumed here to be manufacturing) was shown to follow in most of the usual senses of the term, including a fall in manufacturing output and employment, a worsening of the balance of trade in manufacturing and a fall in the real return to factors specific to the manufacturing sector . . . (p. 841)

This means that it should not be surprising that a decline in manufacturing output has accompanied the growth in oil production. Their analysis is, however, an equilibrium analysis in the sense that there is continuous full employment and a continuous trade balance. What we do not know is how big this adjustment has to be. How much of the fall in manufacturing output and rise in unemployment was actually due to exchange rate overshooting in response to tight monetary policy, as has been emphasised by Buiter and Miller? (1981 a and b) (See Chapter 5.) This is hard to say. But it is clear that the combination of tight monetary policy and North Sea oil was fatal for a significant number of manufacturers.

The policy choices posed by this problem have been analysed by Corden (1981) under the title of 'Exchange Rate Protection.' The presence of a booming sector, like oil, will appreciate the domestic currency. This will make manufacturing less competitive. Should the Government let this appreciation occur, thereby taking the benefits of oil in a terms of trade gain but at the cost of some disruption to manufacturing? Or should it, rather, hold down the exchange rate either by intervention directly (buying dollars) or by expansionary monetary policy (buying bonds or expanding the budget deficit)? There is probably not much the Government could or should do about the equilibrium adjustment. But there is surely a case for policies which offset any tendency for overshooting. There is also a case for policies which recognise the changing employment patterns towards an expansion of services including some of those provided by the public sector.

Summary

Supply shocks are difficult to analyse in the framework of traditional macroeconomic models. There was some confusion about the appropriate response to the 1973 oil price rise. There is also a dangerous tendency among all shades of opinion to discuss the 'solution' to the present difficulties of the UK economy without recognising that it is not an old-style 'macroeconomic' problem. A major influence on the recent evolution of the UK economy has been North Sea oil. Without recognising this as a structural problem there is a serious danger that 'solutions' will be ill-conceived.

10

Macroeconomics in the 1980s

Macroeconomics is in a state of disarray. Economic problems in general are as great as they have ever been. Yet the economics profession manages to sustain voices calling simultaneously for radically different strategies to solve the problems. Much of the diversity of proposed solutions results not from disagreement about goals, but rather from deep disagreement about how the economy works. What is strange, perhaps, in a period of rapidly rising unemployment, is the growth of New Classical economics which assumes that prices adjust to clear markets. The last period of comparable unemployment – in the 1930s – spawned an analysis which presumed market failure. This was Keynesian economics.

Macroeconomics and the Market

It is hard to read Keynes' General Theory without coming away with the impression that he was hinting at an analysis of why markets fail. The debates of the subsequent decades have demonstrated that it is far from clear what the precise nature of that market failure is. Keynesian macroeconomics was developed on the basis of a particular presumption. When some prices (or money wages) are sticky there can be a shortage of aggregate demand. Where aggregate demand is deficient, as evidenced by unemployment, there will be no great benefit from marginal or piecemeal downward adjustments of money wages. This could, indeed, make things worse. The 'solution' is, rather, to engineer an increase in aggregate demand by raising government expenditure or, rather, as

Keynes actually proposed, raising public sector involvement in investment.

The research strategy suggested by the Keynesian analysis was an identification and empirical refinement of the major expenditure categories – consumption, investment, imports, exports etc. Armed with the tools to forecast these expenditures, the deficiency of aggregate demand could be forecast and that deficiency could be made up by the appropriate government budget.

There are many who still view the world this way. The substantial rise in unemployment is taken to be indicative of a major deficiency of aggregate demand. Accordingly, the appropriate policy should be for the government to instigate a substantial reflation by expanding its own expenditure. This expenditure increase should not be financed by taxes, but rather by borrowing. Remarkably, the dominant voices in the United States are making exactly the opposite recommendation for solving unemployment – a reduction in the deficit as a way of lowering real interest rates and increasing private investment.

More importantly for present purposes, there are those who take a radically different view from the Keynesians as to the nature of the market failure which produces unemployment. The market works – including the labour market – except as a result of specific distortions caused by government intervention or by trade unions. Parkin and Bade (1982, Chapter 12), for example, list four causes of unemployment. These are minimum wage laws, trade unions which raise wages, unemployment benefit and distortionary taxes. According to this view, a reduction of government intervention will help to solve the problem since it will free the market of distortion and enable it to work freely. Reducing the powers of trade unions would also help by reducing their ability to raise wages above market clearing levels.

The latter is a perfectly respectable line to take if it is believed that the market would work 'perfectly' in the absence of such distortions. However, it would also seem possible that the market would be at least as imperfect even in the absence of these specific distortions. There are good reasons to believe that labour markets would not be 'flex-price' markets (Okun 1981) even in the absence of these imperfections. The problem for macroeconomics is, therefore, how to explain why employment prospects are better at some times than others, *given* that wages are going to be sluggish in adjusting.

The New Classical economists, such as Robert Lucas, who wish to explain business cycles would not necessarily accept that wages are sluggish, but they are forced to introduce some form of sluggish adjustment in order to explain events. They may, indeed, be forced to accept wage stickiness as a possibility where this is rationally established between optimising individuals. However, their current interpretation of the nature of the market failure responsible for business cycles is very different from the Keynesian diagnosis.

The actor in a New Classical world is rational and well informed up to a point. He has perfect information about the market for his own output, but he only learns about other markets with a lag. The world is stochastic so he acts on the basis of a statistical expectation of the outcome in all other markets. In the aggregate only unexpected money shocks are likely to have general effects (see Chapters 4 and 8) and such shocks will generate cycles if they influence capital formation. Thus, market failure arises from the mistaken price signals caused by *unanticipated* monetary shocks. This suggests that a more stable monetary regime would reduce the problem and enable the market to work efficiently without such distortionary surprises.

There is plenty of evidence that unanticipated inflation is correlated with activity in the way suggested by this line of argument (Batchelor and Sheriff 1980, Holden and Peel 1977). There is also evidence that only unanticipated monetary growth has real effects, as referred to in Chapter 4. Whatever view one takes of this evidence, however, it has certainly not been established that these unanticipated events are sufficiently strong as to explain all the cycles in, say, the British economy. The point at issue is not whether this approach can produce a difference equation of the right order to fit the data – presumably it can. It is, rather, the implication of the theory that systematic stabilisation policy cannot help.

The problem we face in evaluating such implications is that they are not really implications at all but assumptions. If the free market is perfect, even if disturbed by random imperfections, there is going to be little the government can do except to make things worse. A model which presumes this to be the case can only be used to generate implications for government policy if it is first shown that the world really is like this.

This is not to say that New Classical economics is necessarily on the wrong track. But it is as well to remember that if the market really did work well, macroeconomics would be unnecessary.

Macroeconomics and Aggregate Supply

The above disagreements are normally reflected in macroeconomics in discussions of the shape of the aggregate supply curve. Keynesians believe it to be positively sloped; the Classical analysis has it as vertical; Monetarists, in contrast, have it positively sloped in the short run and vertical in the long run. New Classicists have it vertical except for unanticipated demand changes, in which case it is positively sloped. These differences reflect differences in belief about the working of markets, especially the labour market. The Classical labour market clears uniquely with respect to the real wage. Elasticity of supply requires either excess supply (i.e. non-clearing markets) or distortions or asymmetries of some kind. This is market failure.

The aggregate supply curve is a useful analytical device, but there are important respects in which it over-simplifies the characterisation of the economy. Aggregate supply curves reflect the output of the economy modelled as a single homogeneous production sector. This framework is not appropriate for analysing situations where sectoral shifts of production are a central element. Enough difficulty was caused by a major change in the price of an import (oil). But this model is clearly inappropriate as a tool for analysing the effects of the emergence of a major extractive sector (North Sea oil). This is most obvious when stated in the (almost) equivalent form of an expectations augmented Phillips Curve.[1] The expansion of oil output causes a decline in manufacturing production (see Chapter 9). This decline is associated with a rise in unemployment. There is, thus, a break in the previous aggregate relationship between output and employment.

Has the natural rate shifted? In a sense it has because there has been structural change. In another sense it may not have done because we are now in a transition to a new equilibrium employment structure. The natural rate will not be evident again until that new structure is reached – unless, of course, the rate of structural change continues, which is unlikely. In the meantime, inflation-unemployment dynamics will (as we have seen) be in a new dimension. Measured output will also behave in ways not obviously related to traditional aggregate demand measures.

Once the macroeconomic relevance of supply structure is noticed, some comments on government policy suggest themselves. Macroeconomics has always treated 'government' simply as a consumer of the output of the homogeneous private manufacturing sector. In reality, government is itself a producer of goods and services. Even ignoring nationalised industries, this is a sector of significant size (about a quarter of GDP). Keynesian macroeconomics focused entirely upon expenditure (demand) effects of government spending. There are supply side effects too. The crowding out literature has emphasised the wasteful resource use of the public sector (see Chapter 7). However, it is absurd to suggest that a smaller provision of public services is always better than the current level. Indeed, the analysis of Corden and Neary (1982) (see Chapter 9) suggests that the opposite is the case following a boom in oil production. The service sector should expand both because extra services will be demanded and because labour released from manufacturing will not find employment in oil extraction. Public sector services such as health and education are no exception.

There should be more to supply side economics than insinuations about the incentive effects of taxation. Many public sector activities are both directly productive and indirectly productive through their beneficial effect on private sector productivity. This is not the place to pursue this argument much further, but it should be obvious that even if a case is made for cutting public sector consumption on macroeconomic grounds, it requires a different case to justify cutting public sector production. Needless to say, governments have not made this distinction and, as a result, have often made most cuts in exactly these areas where the public sector is most productive. Public investment since 1976 is a case in point.

The World Economy

There is only a limited amount that can be achieved by analysing an economy like the UK in ignorance of what is going on in the rest of the world. External forces could be relegated to a subsidiary role in the 1950s and early 1960s because there was stable growth at low inflation rates. There were no dramatic swings in terms of trade, and exchange rates were generally pegged. This is the kind of world in which a Keynesian expenditure-type system is likely to perform most adequately as a macro-model.

The deterioration in the world economy – slower growth, higher inflation, big terms of trade swings – certainly has had its impact upon the British economy. However, while some economies always appear to do a bit better than par – Japan, West Germany, Switzerland – by most indicators, Britain always seems to do somewhat worse. Politicians, naturally enough, try to blame the worst effects of their policies on world events, implicitly out of their control. Economists should not be fooled by such claims. Inflation need not have been as high as it was in 1975 and unemployment need not have been as high as it was in 1983. The reader who does not accept this should go back to the beginning of this book and read it again.

A significant change in the world environment since the early 1970s has been the switch from fixed to floating exchange rates for the major industrial countries. Many prominent economists in the 1960s advocated a move to floating rates as a way of eliminating the growth constraint imposed by the balance of payments. There has been virtually no growth in Britain in the decade since floating. Much of this deterioration must be associated with the disruptive effects of exchange rate swings as well as the policy swings which floating permits. Oil prices and oil production are obviously important – especially the latter in the UK case – but it seems reasonable to associate the general swings in activity at the world level primarily with monetary disturbances. The excessive expansion of 1970–73 and the excessive contraction of 1980–83 are at least clear cut. These were led by policies in the USA.

It does not seem likely that the clock can be turned back to the early 1960s. However, it is to be hoped that the disturbances of the 1980s will be less severe than those of the 1970s. In any event, the policy makers in each country need to be alert to world developments. These may not influence their economies in simple and obvious ways which can be offset by a wave of a wand, but influence their economies they will. Solutions to problems will depend on the cause and not merely upon the symptoms.

British Macroeconomics

At the time of writing (April 1983) there is a general election approaching. This may lead to a continuance of present Conservative policies or it may lead to the alternative strategy of the Labour Party being adopted. Neither prospect is without obvious pitfalls. What is clear, however, is that macroeconomists of all persuasions have no reason to be complacent about the reliability of their own expertise in the area. The challenge is to demonstrate the error of those whose views support policy recommendations which may appear dangerous. The student, it is to be hoped, will be critical of what is taught. But do not lose sight of the importance of the questions. The stakes are high.

Note

1 The Phillips Curve is $p = \alpha(\bar{U} - U) + p^e$. The supply curve is $Y = \bar{Y} + \beta(p - p^e)$ where p is inflation, Y output and U unemployment. If there is a direct relation between employment and output, these are equivalent. Notice, however, that the Phillips Curve was conceived as a disequilibrium relationship. The supply curve is not.

References

Alt, J. and Chrystal, K. A. (1983) *Political Economics*, University of California Press/Wheatsheaf.
Andersen, L. C. and Jordan, J. L. (1968) 'Monetary and fiscal actions: a test of their relative importance in economic stabilization', *Federal Reserve Bank of St. Louis Monthly Review*, November.
Artis, M. J. and Lewis, M. K. (1976) 'The demand for money in the UK 1963-1973', *Manchester School*.
Attfield, C. L. F., Demery, D. and Duck, N. W. (1981) 'A quarterly model of unanticipated monetary growth, output and the price level in the UK 1963-78', *Journal of Monetary Economics*, November.
Azariadis, C. (1975) 'Implicit contracts and under-employment equilibria', *Journal of Political Economy*, 3, December.
Bacon, R. and Eltis, W. (1976) *Britain's Economic Problem: Too Few Producers*, Macmillan.
Baily, M. N. (1974) 'Wages and employment under uncertain demand', *Review of Economic Studies*, Vol. 41.
Barro, R. J. (1977) 'Unanticipated money growth and unemployment in the US', *American Economic Review*, March.
Barro, R. J. (1978) 'Unanticipated money, output and the price level in the US', *Journal of Political Economy*, August.
Barro, R. J. and Grossman, H. (1976) *Money, Employment and Inflation*, Cambridge University Press.
Batchelor, R. and Sheriff, T. D. (1980) 'Unemployment and unanticipated inflation in post-war Britain', *Economica*, May.
Batten, D. S. and Hafer, R. W. (1983) 'The relative impact of monetary and fiscal actions on economic activity: a cross country comparison', *Federal Reserve Bank of St. Louis Review*, January.
Begg, D. K. H. (1982) *The Rational Expectations Revolution in Macroeconomics*, Philip Allan.
Brunner, K. and Meltzer, A. H. (1976) 'Government, the private sector and "crowding out"', *The Banker*, July, pp. 765-769.
Buiter, W. and Miller, M. (1981a) 'The Thatcher experiment: the first two years', *Brooking Papers on Economic Activity*, Part 2.

Buiter, W. and Miller, M. (1981b) 'Monetary policy and international competitiveness: the problems of adjustment', in W. Eltis and P. J. N. Sinclair (eds), *The Money Supply and the Exchange Rate*, Oxford University Press.

Carlson, K. M. and Spencer, R. W. (1975) 'Crowding out and its critics', *Federal Reserve Bank of St. Louis Monthly Review*, December.

Chrystal, K. A. and Alt, J. (1979) 'Endogenous government behaviour: Wagner's Law or Gotterdamerung?', in P. M. Jackson and S. T. Cook (eds), *Current Issues in Fiscal Policy*, Martin Robertson.

Chrystal, K. A. and Alt, J. (1981) 'Public sector behaviour: the status of the political business cycle', in D. Currie, R. Nobay and D. Peel (eds), *Macroeconomic Analysis Essays in Macroeconomics and Econometrics*, Croom Helm.

Clower, R. (1965) 'The Keynesian counter-revolution: a theoretical appraisal', in F. H. Hahn and F. P. R. Brechling (eds), *The Theory of Interest Rates*, Macmillan.

Corden, W. M. (1981) 'Exchange rate protection', in R. N. Cooper *et. al.* (eds), *The International Monetary System Under Flexible Exchange Rates: Global, Regional and National*, Ballinger, Cambridge, Massachusetts.

Corden, W. M. and Neary, J. P. (1982) 'Booming sector and de-industrialization in a small open economy', *Economic Journal*, December.

Dornbusch, R. (1976a) 'The theory of flexible exchange rate regimes and macroeconomic policy', *Scandinavian Journal of Economics*, Vol. 78, No. 2.

Dornbusch, R. (1976b) 'Expectations and exchange rate dynamics', *Journal of Political Economy*, Vol. 84, No. 6.

Eltis, W. and Sinclair, P. J. N. (eds) (1981) *The Money Supply and the Exchange Rate*, Oxford University Press.

Fischer, I. (1926, 1973) 'A statistical relation between unemployment and price changes', *International Labour Review*. Reprinted in *Journal of Political Economy*, March/April, pp. 596–602.

Fischer, S. (1977) 'Long-term contracts, rational expectations, and the optimal money supply rule', *Journal of Political Economy*, February.

Frenkel, J. A. (1979) 'On the Mark', *American Economic Review*, September.

Frenkel, J. A. and Johnson, H. G. (eds) (1976) *The Monetary Approach to the Balance of Payments*, George Allen and Unwin.

Frenkel, J. A. and Johnson, H. G. (eds) (1978) *The Economics of Exchange Rates*, Addison-Wesley.

Frey, B. (1978) *Modern Political Economy*, Martin Robertson.

Frey, B. and Schneider, F. (1978) 'A politico-economic model of the UK', *Economic Journal*, June.

Friedman, M. (1968) 'The role of monetary policy', *American Economic Review*, March.

Friedman, M. and Schwartz, A. J. (1963a) 'Money and business cycles', *Review of Economics and Statistics*, Supplement, pp. 32–64.

REFERENCES 175

Friedman, M. and Schwartz, A. J. (1963b) *A Monetary History of the US 1867-1960*, New York, NBER.

Friedman, M. and Schwartz, A. J. (1982) *Monetary Trends in the US and UK*, University of Chicago Press.

Goldfeld, S. and Blinder, A. (1972) 'Some implications of endogenous stabilisation policy', *Brooking Papers on Economic Activity*, Part 3.

Gordon, R. A. (1961) *Business Fluctuations*, Harper and Bros. New York, second edition.

Gordon, R. J. (1978) *Macroeconomics*, Little Brown, Boston.

Grossman, J. and Hart, O. D. (1981) 'Implicit contracts, moral hazard and unemployment', *AEA Papers and Proceedings*, May.

Hansen, A. (1953) *A Guide to Keynes*, McGraw-Hill.

Harrod, R. F. (1936) *The Trade Cycle: An Essay*, Oxford University Press.

Hendry, D. F. and Mizon, G. E. (1978) 'Serial correlation as a convenient simplification, not a nuisance', *Economic Journal*, September.

Henry, S. G. B. and Ormerod, P. A. (1978) 'Incomes policy and wage inflation: empirical evidence for the UK 1961-1977', *NIESR Economics Review*, August, pp. 31-39.

Hicks, J. R. (1937) 'Mr Keynes and the Classics, a suggested interpretation', *Econometrica*, April.

Hicks, J. R. (1950) *A Contribution to the Theory of the Trade Cycle*, Oxford University Press.

Hicks, J. (1974) *The Crisis in Keynesian Economics*, Basil Blackwell.

Hines, A. G. (1964) 'Trade unions and wage inflation in the UK 1893-1960', *Review of Economic Studies*, pp. 221-52.

Hines, A. G. and Catephores, G. (1970) 'Investment in UK manufacturing industry', in K. Hilton and D. F. Heathfield (eds) *The Econometric Study of the UK*, Macmillan.

Holden, K. and Peel, D. A. (1977) 'Unemployment and unanticipated inflation', *European Economic Review*, Vol. 10.

Jackson, P. M. and Cook, S. T. (eds) (1979) *Current Issues in Fiscal Policy*, Martin Robertson.

Johnson, H. G. (1976) 'The monetary approach to balance of payments theory', in J. A. Frenkel and H. G. Johnson (eds) *The Monetary Approach to the Balance of Payments*, George Allen and Unwin.

Jonson, P. (1976) 'A model of the UK balance of payments', *Journal of Political Economy*, Vol. 84, No. 5.

Keynes, J. M. (1936) *The General Theory of Employment, Interest and Money*, Macmillan.

Laidler, D. E. W. (1976) 'Inflation in Britain: a Monetarist perspective', *American Economic Review*, September.

Laidler, D. E. W. (1978) 'Money and money income: an essay on the transmission mechanism', *Journal of Monetary Economics*, April.

Laidler, D. E. W. (1980) 'The demand for money in the US - yet again', in K. Brunner and A. H. Meltzer (eds), *Carnegie-Rochester Conference Series on Public Policy*, Vol. 12, Spring, pp. 219-272.

Laidler, D. E. W. (1982) *Monetarist Perspectives*, Philip Allan.

Laury, J. S. E., Lewis, G. R. and Ormerod, P. A. (1978) 'Properties of

macroeconomic models of the UK economy: a comparative study', *NIESR Economic Review*, February.
Layard, R. (1982) 'Is incomes policy the answer to unemployment?', *Economica*, August.
Leijonhufvud, A. (1968) *On Keynesian Economics and the Economics of Keynes*, Oxford University Press.
Leijonhufvud, A. (1969) 'Keynes and the Classics', *Institute of Economic Affairs Occasional Paper 30*.
Lewis, G. R. and Ormerod, P. A. (1979) 'Policy simulations and model characteristics', in P. M. Jackson and S. T. Cook (eds), *Current Issues in Fiscal Policy*, Martin Robertson.
Lipsey, R. G. (1960) 'The relationship between unemployment and the rate of change of money wage rates in the UK 1862–1957: a further analysis', *Economica*, pp. 1–31.
Lucas, R. E. (1972) 'Expectations and the neutrality of money', *Journal of Economic Theory*, Vol. 5.
Lucas, R. E. (1973) 'Some international evidence on output-inflation trade-offs', *American Economic Review*, Vol. 63.
Lucas, R. E. (1975) 'An equilibrium model of the business cycle, *Journal of Political Economy*, December, pp. 1113–1144.
Lucas, R. E. (1976) 'Econometric policy evaluation: a critique', in K. Brunner and A. H. Meltzer (eds), 'The Phillips Curve and labour markets', supplement to *Journal of Monetary Economics*.
Lucas, R. E. (1977) 'Understanding business cycles', in K. Brunner and A. H. Meltzer (eds), *Stabilization of the Domestic and International Economy*, Carnegie-Rochester Conference Series. Reprinted in Lucas (1981).
Lucas, R. E. (1981) *Studies in Business Cycle Theory*, Basil Blackwell.
Lucas, R. E. and Rapping, L. (1969) 'Real wages, employment and inflation', *Journal of Political Economy*, Vol. 77.
Lucas, R. E. and Sargent, Thomas J. (1981a) 'After Keynesian macroeconomics', in R. E. Lucas and T. J. Sargent (eds), *Rational Expectaions and Econometric Practice*, Ch. 16, George Allen and Unwin.
Lucas, R. E. and Sargent, T. J. (eds) (1981b) *Rational Expectations and Econometric Practice*, George Allen and Unwin.
Macrae, E. (1977) 'A political model of the business cycle', *Journal of Political Economy*, Vol. 85, No. 2.
Malinvaud, E. (1977) *The Theory of Unemployment Reconsidered*, Basil Blackwell.
Matthews, R. C. O. (1959) *The Trade Cycle*, Nisbet and Cambridge.
Meade, J. E. and Andrews, P. W. S. (1951) 'Summary of replies to questions on the effects of interest rates', in T. Wilson and P. W. S. Andrews (eds), *Oxford Studies in the Price Mechanism*, Oxford University Press.
Miller, M. H. (1976) 'Can a rise in import prices be inflationary and deflationary', *American Economic Review*, September.
Mitchell, W. C. (1941) *Business Cycles and Their Causes*, University of California Press.

REFERENCES

Modigliani, F. (1944) 'Liquidity preference and the theory of interest and money', *Econometrica*, January.
Modigliani, F. (1977) 'The Monetarist controversy or should we forsake stabilization policy?', *American Economic Review*, March.
Mundell, R. A. (1968) *International Economics*, Macmillan.
Muth, J. F. (1961) 'Rational expectations and the theory of price movements', *Econometrica*, July.
Nordhaus, W. (1975) 'The political business cycle', *Review of Economic Studies*, Vol. 42.
Okun, A. M. (1981) *Prices and Quantities: A Macroeconomic Analysis*, Basil Blackwell.
Parkin, M. (1978) 'Alternative explanations of UK inflation: a survey', in M. Parkin and M. T. Sumner (eds), *Inflation in the UK*, Manchester University Press.
Parkin, M. and Bade, R. (1982) *Modern Macroeconomics*, Philip Allan.
Parkin, M. and Sumner, M. T. (eds) (1972) *Incomes Policy and Inflation*, Manchester University Press.
Parkin, M., Sumner, M. T. and Jones, R. A. (1972) 'A survey of the econometric evidence of the effects of incomes policy on the rate of inflation', in M. Parkin and M. T. Sumner (eds), *Incomes Policy and Inflation*, Manchester University Press.
Parkin, M. and Sumner, M. T. (eds) (1978) *Inflation in the UK*, Manchester University Press.
Phelps, E. S. (1968) 'Money-wage dynamics and labour market equilibrium', *Journal of Political Economy*, July/August.
Phillips, A. W. H. (1958) 'The relation between unemployment and the rate of change of money-wage rates in the UK, 1861-1957', *Economica*, November, pp. 283-99.
Purdy, D. L. and Zis, G. (1973) 'Trade unions and wage inflation in the UK: a re-appraisal', in M. Parkin (ed.), *Essays in Modern Economics*, Longman.
Samuelson, P. (1939) 'Interactions between the multiplier analysis and the principle of acceleration', *Review of Economics and Statistics*, Vol. 21.
Sargent, T. (1976) 'The observational equivalence of natural and unnatural rate theories of macroeconomics', *Journal of Political Economy*, Vol. 84, No. 3.
Sargent, T. J. and Wallace, N. (1975) 'Rational expectations, the optimal monetary instrument and the optimal money supply rule', *Journal of Political Economy*, April.
Savage, D. (1978) 'The channels of monetary influence: a survey of the empirical evidence', *NIESR Economic Review*, February.
Schumpeter, J. (1939) *Business Cycles: a Theoretical, Historical and Statistical Analysis of the Capitalist Process*, McGraw-Hill.
Spencer, R. W. and Yohe, W. P. (1970) 'The crowding out of private expenditures by fiscal policy actions', *Federal Reserve Bank of St. Louis Monthly Review*, October.
Sumner, M. T. (1978) 'Wage Determination', in M. Parkin and M. T. Sumner (eds), *Inflation in the UK*, Manchester University Press.

Taylor, J. B. (1979) 'Staggered wage setting in a macroeconomic model', *American Economic Review*, Papers and Proceedings, Vol. 69.

Taylor, J. B. (1980) 'Aggregate dynamics and staggered contracts', *Journal of Political Economy*, Vol. 88.

Townend, J. C. (1976) 'The personal saving ratio', *Bank of England Quarterly Bulletin*, March.

Tufte, E. (1978) *The Political Control of the Economy*, Princeton University Press.

Wilson, T. and Andrews, P. W. S. (1951) *Oxford Studies in the Price Mechanism*, Oxford University Press.

Public Expenditure Committee, Ninth Report (1974). Session 1974, HC328, HMSO, July.

Index

Aggregate demand, 15–21, 23, 109–111
Aggregate supply, 15–21, 75–78, 109–111, 169
Alt, J. E., 64, 129, 130, 140, 141, 156, 157
Andersen, L. C., 130
Andrews, P. W. S., 32
Artis, M. J., 57
Attfield, C. L. F., 81
Azariadis, C., 125

Bacon, R., 138–139
Bade, R., 18, 167
Baily, M. N., 125
Balance of payments, 87–95
    Keynesian approach, 87–89
    Monetary approach, 92–95
Barber, A., 35, 62, 71
Barro, R., 38, 81
Batchelor, K., 118, 168
Batten, D. S., 130
Begg, D. K. H., 3
Blinder, A., 130
Brunner, K., 136
Buiter, W., 4, 136
Business cycles, 75, 142–157

Cambridge equation, 49
Callaghan, J., 27, 118
Carlson, K. M., 130, 132
Catephores, G., 32
Chrystal, K. A., 64, 129, 130, 140, 141, 156, 157
Clower, R., 36–37
Competition and credit control, 35, 62, 71
Corden, M., 164, 165, 170
Crowding out, 129–141

Demery, D., 81
Dornbusch, R., 4, 99, 101
Duck, N. W., 81

Eltis, W., 99, 100, 138–9
Exchange rate, 62–63, 95–106
Expectations, 67, 72–74, 78
    Rational, 3–4, 67–69, 74, 79

Fischer, S., 81
Fisher, I., 107
Frankel, J., 100
Frenkel, J., 96
Friedman, M., 49, 50, 53, 61, 63, 64, 109, 130, 146–148

Goldfeld, S., 130
Gordon, R. A., 144
Gordon, R. J., 110
Grossman, H., 38
Grossman, S., 125

Hafer, R. W., 130
Hansen, A., 27

Harrod, R., 146
Hart, O., 125
Hawtrey, R., 146
Hayek, F. V., 63
Healey, D., 63
Hendry, D. F., 57
Henry, S. G. B., 126
Hicks, J. R., 11, 144, 146, 152
Hines, A., 32, 109
Holden, K., 168

Incomes policy, 125–128
Inflation, 58–63, 107–124
IS-LM model, 11–15, 22–23, 30, 49–50, 89–91, 131–133

Johnson, H. G., 93–94, 96
Jones, R. A., 125
Jonson, P., 54
Jordan, J. L., 130

Keynes, J. M., 11, 31, 32, 33, 36, 38, 52, 78, 146, 166
Keynesian economics, 3, 8–11, 21–47, 69, 129, 144–146, 153–154, 159–163, 166–170

Layard, R., 127
Leijonhufvud, A., 36–37
Lewis, G. R., 136
Lewis, M. K., 57
Lipsey, R. G., 107
Lucas, R. E., 6, 68, 69, 75–78, 80, 136, 142, 144, 148–154, 168
Lucas Critique, 6, 70–72

Macrae, D., 156
Malinvaud, E., 38–40
Matthews, R. C. O., 144, 146
Meade, J., 32
Meltzer, A., 136
Miller, M., 4, 158–161, 165
Mitchell, W. C., 143
Mizon, G., 57
Modigliani, F., 32, 142
Monetarism, 3, 5, 21, 35–36, 48–65, 146–148
Monetary policy, 34, 60–63, 148, 153–4

Ineffectiveness, 78–82
Money demand, 12, 14, 55–57
Multiplier, 28, 31, 38, 70, 137–138
Mundell, R., 89
Muth, J., 74

Natural rate hypothesis, 66, 113–114
Neary, P., 164, 170
New Classical macroeconomics, 3–5, 18, 21, 52, 55, 66–83, 142, 148–154, 166–170
Nixon, R., 27, 62
Nordhaus, W., 154
North Sea oil, 104, 123, 158, 164–165, 169

Okun, A., 124, 152, 167
Ormerod, P., 126, 136

Parkin, J. M., 18, 125, 167
Peel, D. A., 168
Phelps, E. S., 109
Phillips, A. W., 107
Phillips curve, 35, 61, 107–109, 111–114, 154–155, 169
Pigou, A. C., 49
Pigou effect, 52
Political business cycles, 154–157
Political Monetarism, 63–64
PSBR, 51
Purdy, D., 107

Quantity theory, 48–49, 58–60

Rapping, L., 75–76, 150
Rational expectations, 3–4, 67–69, 74, 79
Reagan, R., 27, 48, 63
Real balance effect, 52–54
Robertson, D. H., 49

Samuelson, P., 144
Sargent, T., 69, 70, 80, 149, 152
Savage, D., 32
Schumpeter, J., 143
Schwartz, A., 146–148
Sheriff, T. D., 118, 168
Sinclair, P. J. N., 99, 100

Spencer, R. W., 130, 132
Stabilisation policy, see Business cycles
Sumner, M., 118, 125

Taylor, J., 81
Thatcher, M., 27, 48, 63, 118
Townend, J. C., 54
Tufte, E., 154

Unemployment, 3, 29, 33, 38, 40–47, 107–128

Wallace, N., 80
Walras' Law, 37
Worswick, G. D. N., 159

Yohe, W. P., 130

Zis, G., 109